Sacred Verses

Entering the Labyrinth of the Gods

Ptahmassu K.M. Nofra-Uaa

Icons of Kemet
Words for Eternity

www.iconsofkmt.com

Sacred Verses – Entering the Labyrinth of the Gods
©2016 Ptahmassu K.M. Nofra-Uaa
ISBN 978-1-7376610-0-9

Cover art ©2014 Ptahmassu K.M. Nofra-Uaa

Printed in cooperation with
Lulu Enterprises, Inc.
860 Aviation Parkway, Suite 100
Morrisville, NC 27560

9 781737 661009

Table of Contents

Dedication

To our Ancient and Eternal Gods,
You Who came before us in the primordial ocean of time,
Who transcend time, age, and mortality,
You Who came before our flesh and blood,
and yet gave birth to these, which pass away and return,
You Who preceded the human race,
and yet are the Mothers and Fathers of all its generations,
You Who have been known before religion was conceived,
Who exist outside belief, thought, and philosophy,
You Who challenge the myopic and the singular,
the authoritarian and the jealous,
You Whose wisdom is measured through the Mysteries,
Whose forms are comprehended though the diverse and the
plural, the Many and the All,

To our Ancient Ancestors and Victorious Dead,
To all those who have carried the sacred torch of Memory
before us,
Who have heard the call of the Gods and answered,
and passed down that recognition as the inheritance of
humankind,
Who have maintained the holy ties of offering and sacrifice,
and given the fields of the Earth their due as our divine
sustenance,
Who have remembered the stories of our Gods,
and bequeathed these to their children who followed after,
To all those whose prayers and sacrifices have maintained

the open doors between our world and the Sacred reality,
To those bards, poets, philosophers, and sibyls
who received the shouts or whispers of our Gods,
and left imprints in the sands of history
to be read and recited by all who came after.

Above all, the verses that follow are a testimony to the
immutable and everlasting presence of the Gods, traditions, and
voices of polytheism,
Whose sacred embers are being fanned and revived by
contemporary initiates,
May the merits of this volume belong to them and their
devotion,
To all those who adore the living Gods and seek to engage in
Their service.

Acknowledgements

I must express my love and gratitude to my husband Brent Fraser for his unbreakable faith in this and all work in which I am engaged. He has provided the backbone from which these verses have manifested, and, through his wisdom and insight, has helped me to grow in my love for sacred language as a tool for spiritual transformation in our world.

Dr. Tamara Siuda deserves recognition for her very generous support of my work and aims, for offering her valuable time to kindly inform or reinforce my studies as a Kemetic and devotional polytheist. Dr. Siuda was never too busy (though in reality she was *more than busy!)* to hunt down source texts or academic papers for some obscure facet of my research, and even further to provide deep insights from her areas of expertise, which are quite broad in scope and extremely valuable to one without academic credentials. I am especially thankful for her fellowship and deep love for the Gods.

I am very grateful for the sacred friendship and camaraderie of Setken of Melbourne, the "Nouveau Kemetic" painter whose presence has touched my life profoundly with his fascination for all things Kemetic, and authentic devotion to the Gods. Setken has played a significant role in my development as a Kemetic iconographer, and it was through his zealous belief in my devotional poetry that I was able to arrive at a place of confidence in my placing my work out in the open for the world.

Setken's passion and wild commitment to pushing through boundaries in order to reach the Gods has shaped my life as a polytheist, and I know that my evolution as a sacred artist has only been enhanced through his honest friendship.

My sincere thanks to Dagulf Loptson for her dear friendship and encouragement, without which this book would not have made it to publication as this time. Hers were the words of advice, paired with determined guidance, that cut through my apprehension and compelled me to see the importance of seeking publication for my work. I am grateful to her for her dedication to my vision, and also for being an honest friend at a time when that alone could make or break my spirit.

A note of gratitude must go out to Lo, founder of Numen Arts, and a much respected peer in the polytheist revival community, for his exceptional book Art & Numen (2020), which appeared at a time when I needed to see the possibilities of a polytheist revival movement through the sacred arts. Lo has formulated a powerful manifesto for polytheist artists today, one that has the ability to be realized because of its clarity and applicability to the struggles and issues faced by creative hands enthused with love for the Gods.

Lastly, but certainly not least, I pay tribute to my mother and thank her for her fervent belief in my obsession as a writer. Hers has always been an unbending certainty that my poetry was of value and something to be followed. Though I had my doubts and my moments of rebellion against my gifts, she never lost faith in me nor ceased to voice her support for my writing.

Although the subject matter will conflict with her personal beliefs, I hope that she will recognize the role she has played in bringing this manuscript to fruition.

Ptahmassu K.M. Nofra-Uaa
West Wendover, NV
Full Moon Day
July 24, 2021

Introduction

"I turn from this earth over which living men wander,
to find pleasures and senses that can never be filled,
green youth that fades, riches and praise,
that stand for as long as a blade of grass stands.
They are all cut down by that indomitable wind
that drives the swallows before him.
This is what I am, and what you are, and what we are,
meeting the sky again after our journey,
where there is never again a thing to fear."

(39, *I Slay Death In His Field*)

This is a book about death and darkness, about stagnation and decay, about wading through the mud of grasping and desire, about being stripped of one's flesh and illusions, about the process of deconstructing our mortality. It is also a book about life and illumination, discovering in one's deepest desires the path to liberation, finding the Gods as the ultimate reality, a reality in which death and decay are the building blocks for immortality. In short, this is a book about *initiation*, the psychospiritual process of connecting the adept to personal gnosis. Personal gnosis cannot be arrived at through the cerebral faculties alone, it must arise through an immediate and personal spiritual experience through which one becomes aware of one's relationship to the Sacred. This is a dangerous process, and one our ego will resist with all its might.

Adepts of all mystical traditions know that initiation is a form of death. The person we think we are, the *self* our ego clings to like a lover, falls, transforms, or is transmuted into something new. We recognize our nakedness in the presence of the Gods and Holy Powers, our wetness, our newness as beings coming once more into the world of the senses. Initiation is a form of self-deconstruction, chopping away at the bits and pieces of the *self* until we are faced with the corpse of our old personality. What do we do then? We clothe ourselves in a new body that speaks to us of reconstruction and renewal, a personality shining and wearing its own darkness with confidence. Our gnosis achieved through initiation is that we are dying each and every moment of our lives, changing our perception of ourselves from moment to moment, and seeing the world as we know it die and fluctuate before our eyes. Impermanence is the gnosis that arises from the most illusion-shattering initiations. What we think is changeless, is as stable as the shifting sand beneath our feet.

What then of the Gods and Holy Powers? Why do we need Them *now*, and how can we find confirmation of our own immortality through Them? These are the questions I asked myself as a child raised in a strict Christian family, raised to accept the physical reality of God and the Devil, the holy war between Christ and Satan, the inevitability of death and Hell as the wages of sin, and the literal, infallible truth of the Gospels. The world as we knew it was the domain of Lucifer and his kin, the souls of all those whose names had not been written in the Book of Life. What I was taught was that my very body and desires were the weapons played by the Devil to enslave my soul. To possess my soul was the root of the battle being waged between God and the Fallen One. To question the literal truth of the Gospels, even for one moment, was to become a disciple of the Devil and a fallen one, for it was not works that could save or condemn humankind, but our beliefs. There was the truth, the Bible as the infallible and inerrant word of God, and there was the great lie, that there is any truth outside the Gospels, that there is any other belief that can be a road to eternal life. Suffering? That is the recompense for straying from the path of the Christian righteous. There is no life or spiritual existence outside the truth of the Gospels.

But something in my conscience spoke out against this indoctrination very early in my childhood. I questioned the very foundation of the Christian doctrine as it was taught to me, that there is only one God and Jesus Christ is indivisible from him as the only savior and redeemer of humankind. My conscience knew this to be untrue, and there was something else in its place, something I refer to as *memory*, and which forms the basis for so much I've recorded in the *Sacred Verses*. This memory is the presence of beliefs and experiences deep in our psyche that preexists our exploration of the ideas they embody. Sitting in church as a boy, I remember asking myself where the *others* were, those *others* who were here long before the Christian God arrived, the *others* who haunted my dreams and pulled on the strings of my heart. Even as a young child I knew that the Gods existed and were the original sources of humankind's spiritual life. My *memory* told me that long before my ancestors had adopted the Christian doctrine they knew the Gods and venerated Them. Everyone alive had ancestors that once lived what we call *paganism*.

Sacred Verses is a journey through one's own past and present towards the reclamation of what I call *polytheistic memory*, or simply *memory* in the verses. This memory is the embodiment of polytheism as the shared experience of the human race prior to the advent of monotheism, and in particular evangelical Christianity. Every single person on this planet has ancestors, and if one follows one's ancestors back far enough in time, one will find that polytheism is there as the most natural expression of human belief. Through the course of conversions and indoctrination, and indeed the overwhelming acceptance of monotheism as the most valid model of religious engagement, our societies have all but erased our polytheistic past, and have willingly severed our ties to those ancient gods that fueled the advent of human societies and civilizations from the beginning. There are societies in the present that have maintained their indigenous traditions and original gods. India with Her *Sanatana Dharma* has withstood the onslaught of monotheistic conversion, remaining a beacon for those who recognize the wisdom of pluralism, coexistence of diverse philosophies and theologies, and unashamed devotion to the revelation of many gods. Can we in the West not drink from the breast of Mother India in order to taste the beginnings of our own spiritual yearnings?

That yearning is so often expressed in the Sacred Verses, the yearning of the suffering human soul begging to be reunited with its Numinous source. The Gods are that numinosity, says the Sacred Verses, they are the preeminent expressions of life and consciousness from Whom we draw breath and experience. Their experience is also our experience through the vehicle of *memory*, which can be accessed by anyone at any time. For memory is the unseen thread that connects us to all that has been experienced before. Our darkness, our unconsciousness is but a knot on a thread tied to the Gods when They existed as seeds of possibility in the primeval body of the Uncreated. Such unconsciousness was once the state of all principles and beings before they became manifest in creation. To become fully conscious, fully aware, awake beings, we must strip the illusions from our eyes and see the phenomenon of life for what it is.

This is the aim of all spiritual traditions and mystical paths, to arrive at a personal gnosis that is substantiated through direct experience. Each direct experience that informs our awakening becomes an initiation into the Mysteries of the Gods, Whose world is the watery, fluid world glimpsed through the veil of religious and spiritual ecstasy. Religious engagement is the horse we ride through the spheres of influence inhabited by our gods. This religious engagement, not being the institutions of organized religion or inflexible doctrine, but rather the framework provided by traditions that offer a means for touching the Holy Powers directly and drawing personal gnosis from Them.

So here we have the Sacred Verses, a set of mystical poems I composed before the Sun rose each morning and the need for more sleep still tugged at my eyelids. These are *memories* rising from dreams occurring in the sleep state, where the Gods and Holy Powers hold sway, and where the initiate is drawn into the darkness from whence we came. These are the products of what we might call *religious ecstasy*, for my writing always began with an exercise of meditation and focus on the personalities of the Gods. *Which Gods?* People who know me primarily through my Kemetic work will be surprised to hear that it was not only the Deities of Kemet Who answered my yearning to set down the journey of the initiate, but rather the deities, demons, and powers of traditions far beyond the borders of the Two Lands, and Powers unnamed in the Verses. These are not the embodiment of a specific tradition or spiritual framework, but rather the Powers of each unique reader desiring to make contact with the spheres of the Gods. Each reader will come to the table with their own experience and aims, and these are honored by the Verses which seek to allow the individual to enter the road required by their individual conscience. There is a freedom in such an approach that is pluralistic in nature and encouraging of pluralism. There is always more than one *right* answer at a time. There are more approaches than there are readers. Monotheism being the exclusion of the Many in favor of the one, these verses champion the alternative approach, that being the existence of the Many in favor of inclusiveness, from which personal gnosis of the All can flourish.

Finally, Sacred Verses is a gathering of magical utterances that pair with the construction of a practice in which workings become the activities of the adept and the Gods coming together for the purpose of co-creation. The adept walks with the Gods, works *for* the Gods, becoming the hands and feet of the Holy Powers in the material world. The invocations summon the ideals of the highest magic, to bring the Numinous and the material together in harmony transcending the perception of physical barriers. The Verses tear down the illusion that the

Sacred and the *profane* are separate. They are, in fact, two sides of the same coin which the adept holds in the palm of their hand. The Gods are the expressions of a conscious creation, ever-expanding and ever creating itself. We are the extensions of that continuous creation, for which the Sacred Verses give gratitude and ecstatic celebration.

Ptahmassu Nofra-Uaa
West Wendover, NV
July 24, 2021

1: Pilgrimage to the Ancestors

Hear the voice of my heart
in the ears of your heart,
a token of my blood
traversing its mortal course,
down through the veins
of our tree of generations.
My pilgrimage sounds with
the coming of twilight,
whose fingers pull forth shadows
like a cowl about my head.

Those who came before me, Hail!
Lift shadow where it falls
at the command of my voice,
which summons the Gods.

Those Gods dwelling in the world below,
open ways for those who serve in silence.
The grave makes Ancestors of us all,
placing silence in the mouth of the verbose.

I travel with a quieted heart,
placing deft fingers around its valves.
I still its wild music,
soothing it into a dove's cooing.
Be still my throbbing drum,
and may furtive action permit us an entry
into the Mysteries of the world below.

Earth, I hear you in the passage of my footsteps.
Sky, tempting the mountains to stretch their legs,
I feel your constellations flickering beneath my skin.
Mortality, you are my bedfellow,
whose lips and lusty promises beckon me
deep down into my grave.

Gods of Old, I couple myself with You,
for You are the true beginning of humankind.
The one may have followed You,
stripped You of Your noble clothing.
But even without a crown,
a king's bearing proclaims his ancestry,
and his subjects still bow before him in awe.
Thus You cannot be forgotten,
nor secreted away within the angry folds of time.

Gods hear me,
and may my prayers be succor for my travels.
A flame I light with my heart in my hand,
traveling through my mortal flesh,
lighting my skin with the breath of the Gods.
O flame, my guide, may my heart speak true.
For the Gods eat only truth,
and digest only devotion.

In this pathway are the haughty trampled,
the boastful stung into silence,
and the vain captured by the net of time.

For the devoted,
the Gods give back their offering manifold,
two doves in the palm of a hand
being the equal of an eagle.
From the loins of a single star flows the seed of millions,
whose lights shatter the indigo veil
as it grasps the Earth in its embrace.
If I give silver, then gold shall crown my head.
If I give my flesh, then a spirit body shall be forged
upon the anvil of the Eternal.

Ancestors, You are the stars in the night sky,
traversing for me the paths of Eternity.
These are the profits of those who follow
in the footsteps of the Gods.
While those who deny Them,
are unheard by the ears of Eternity,
and fade like the shadows
before the noble feet of the Sun.

O Gods, I come forth
with my heart in my hand.
O Gods, receive me!
O Ancestors, I come forth
with Your heart in my hand.
May I follow in Your footsteps!
O Gods, I summon You to receive me,
for I am the kin of my Ancestors among You,
Whom You in the fields of the Blessed have received!

O Gods, I open the Gates!
O Ancestors, wide open are the Doors!
My body, the Doors.
My members, the Gates.
My feet, the Holy Path.
I come forth with my heart in my hand!

2: Initiation

The pull of the Sacred Deep,
I enter without sleep.
Congregation of spirits,
they weave the Ancestral fire,
my heart to keep.

What purpose does the Veil serve,
if not to clothe the eyes of mortals,
to disguise the Sacred with a mask,
to make him remember again?

My body is the vessel,
my flesh its holy core.
Into the fiery mold,
my soul the Gods do pour.

Harmony seeks not to diminish,
to merge the All into one.
Instead it seeks to marry,
the weft cannot be undone.

Passing, traveling,
beyond the distant shore,
a boat without a paddle,
a sail to the worlds of yore.

The boat of the Gods passes in and out
from this world into the other.
From Father's seed we spring
then back inside the Mother.

She eats Her children,
just as stars are swallowed,
while the Earth waits to take them,
into His ground that is hallowed.

I am my Father,
when my flesh makes love,
but when my Soul departs,
it flies to Mother above.

O one, I set fire to your dominance,
your anger and your guile.
I put your ego to rest in the Earth,
to make the Old Gods smile.

I dance naked on your grave,
while the heavens drink my flesh.
Into the fire of Becoming,
my eternal Soul does mesh.

Ancient Mother, untamed Father,
my skin, my love, my sleep,
I awaken from my slumber,
my eyes Your sight to keep.

My blood, my bones you carry,
as Sun and Moon do marry,
silver veil gives way to gold,
and my heart is married,
to the Gods of Old.

3: Beyond the Veil

Is it fortuitous that I have climbed
the spire raised high above,
the mortality given me
by the breast of my mother from where I fed,
was nourished,
was given the essence of life
that resolves itself in death?

It is a grateful heart that finds
the door opening to the naked sky,
where the Gods dance upon breaths of fire,
where water and air weave together
the Mystery of life's becoming.

Is it fortuitous that I have seen these things
that mortal form cannot fathom?
Except for the happenstance that Spirits
find their way into our waking dreams,
and it is from these we awake with a start.
We open our eyes to the transience of our skin,
and the ethereal skeleton becomes our possession.

What we thought our flesh possessed
falls away with the grains of sand,
is blown away by the breath of time.
It knows no constancy, save for that
which changes like the tides.

I climbed the spire the Gods set before me,
seeking the early morning light.
A golden net of dew strung between branches,
heralded the Sun-God's return.
I found Him arrayed in shining mountains,
to the east His countenance shone as fire,
a shield, a mirror winking with blinding white light.

I came to the footfall of ages,
beneath those glimmering mountains,
whose crevices and sentinels told of generations
who had come and gone, believed and faded.
Where are they now?

Beneath the Earth,
in hallows abundant with offerings,
seated in the lap of the Gods,
awaiting the ghosts of children and lovers past,
holding onto hope,
that all life continues beyond the tomb.

These things we all do,
and it is fortuitous that we remember.

So I too pass beyond the veil,
where azure light leads
through the tunnel of the ages,
having come from my mother's wet womb,
and before that from my father's warm seed.

There are these gates in mortal life
through which we pass,
his seed, her womb, to crawl, to walk,
to bend over with age, and then to die.
These are the gateways to a new life,
simply waiting on the other side.

It is wise to listen to the counsel of those who
have walked through the door.
Their eyes have seen what we have yet to see,
their ears have heard the Gods,
we have yet to hear.

All naked.
We come through the gate into this world.
Naked we find ourselves when a new life begins.
We possess nothing before,
and nothing after do we carry.

It is folly to believe that the Sun's light will follow
where the Moon is queen of the vault.
Love lives not inside the grave,
but only within the warm heart beating.
This is what makes life a paradise,
not that which comes after.

It is fortuitous that I have climbed
where mortals in their desire never wish to wander
across the threshold of darkness,
where a new life waits for the intrepid wanderer.

4: The Embrace of Death

Death my mother,
my mother, death,
ever-present in our midst,
yet whose face is never fully unveiled.
Suckle me, fresh from the womb,
even as I drink deeply of life
and celebrate its happy gifts.
Your solemn voice is never far
from the proclamation of joy.

I hold closely to your skin in the night,
living seed has filled entrails,
your sweat on my golden skin,
sleek with life in the pallid moonlight.

A star falls millions of miles away,
its trail is seen by eyes this night
who will be in the ground by morning.
And this is the Great Mystery,
since the beginning of time.
How greedy is She who devours all living souls,
who conceives the seed of dead men,
as the black veil of the midnight sky,
swallows whole the illumination of the stars.

Your body has given up its life inside me,
for a time your arms surround me.
These same clinging branches
are cut down and fall tomorrow,
and such is the destiny
of all things kissed by the Sun.

I have departed my skin after twilight,
the cock's crow a memory from ages ago.
Dawn's blessing cannot reach my face
within the hallows of the Earth,
where beings are born again
through the body of Mother-Sky.

Do you have doubts
that this too shall become you?
Were you not once a quickening of seed,
an infant, a crawler, a child, a youth,
a father, a mother, a care-giver... ?
All these things that pass one to the other,
the triumph of dawn
giving way to the bawdy afternoon sun.

These things you become,
each held for a fragile moment
in the weft and warp of time.
One passes through the other,
and neither may be extracted
from its companion.

To know your mother is to know your father.
To be sated is to know yearning.
To reach climax is to lust for pleasure.
To drink deeply is to know thirst.
To achieve satisfaction is to find discontent.
To find perfection is to uncover a crack.
To devour the Sun is to be left
in Moon's omnipresent shadow.
These are the weft and the warp,
whom no mortal may undo.

Thus I shiver without the comfort of my skin,
when life has abandoned me for the Journey.
This is the path all mortals come to,
no matter how high their place in the Sun.

O Gods, your arms about me,
I come to the Mother's arms.
Swallowed by Her indomitable mouth,
I pass through Her milky breasts,
to find my home in Her silver navel.

Thighs of the Moon, I feel your wet plains
and taste your offering upon my tongue.
This is the sanctuary
in which all souls are held fast,
in death as in life.
We passed through this place as babes,
entered it as living mortals,
and as souls, traverse its inviting grip.
It is the answer to all the Mysteries,
thus Death you are my mother,
and Mother you are my death.

O Father-Sun, I behold Your electric pink light,
making love to the horizon,
where mountains lay down their shadows
as offerings to your holy feet.

I rise like the river,
swollen over its banks in flood season,
high on the wind
and the kiss of the sapphire sky.

I drink all of these things as gifts to be savored,
knowing that twilight shall bring the cloak
of the lonely Moon to rest upon my golden shoulders.
Shiver in darkness, you Ancestors and Spirits,
while you wait for the womb of the Mother
in Her sky to open before you.

In the West you find that place
where all mortals are eventually hidden.
They disguise themselves in Her wet embrace,
cloaked from the recognition
of those they leave behind.

Is it a brothel then,
where all souls who can afford
are bestowed with favors for a time?
She receives them all,
but not as lover.
Time is not a courtesan,
discriminating between affluent or poor.
Death's favors belong to all,
and all become Her guests in that place
of the final Mysteries.

So I come to this path
where all souls come,
and now it may be said that my life is undone.
I have kissed and I have embraced
all the places of Gods and mortals.
Into the mouth of the West
my soul finds embrace again.

5: The Eternal Twining

Your light poured into me
like a pitcher of water.
Envisage twin mountains in the East,
whereupon whose crests dawn's molten glow
suffuses the shadows with life.
It is all a miracle when it takes one by surprise,
when the heart has existed silently as a seed
buried beneath a verdant pasture.

Beloved, there is this Mystery through which I walk,
one foot planted before the other,
delicately seeking out bursts of the Soul
traipsing among the shadows.

A little wren came and landed on my shoulder
his face was my face, his shade my shade.
He came as a reminder,
alighting where apprehension draws one away
from the uncomfortable presence of the Truth.
How fragile is our mortal life,
and how eternal our Soul.

Wren, little wren, I came to hold you close to my breast,
like a lover when dawn strikes
after a night of ecstatic endeavor.
I press your wings close.
These are the flight of Spirit from matter.
I hear your playful melody.
This is the song of a soul in flight from its confinement.
Though do we know how we are confined,
until the moment of our release?

Your love poured into me,
like an ancient song from a plaintive harp.
It sailed straight through me,
a longboat slicing into the frigid waters of a fjord.
What adventurers we are
when all tethers are cut loose,
ropes called logic, reason, and sanity itself.
Is this what the Mysteries demand?

You discovered that cave,
held fast to the valves of my heart,
where no god or spirit or demon could venture.
I bolted the doors,
living only through my flesh.

This is the skin of my mother, longing.
These are the eyes of my father,
devouring everything in their sight.
This is the seed of my father's father,
from whom generations have been spun.

I have never been alone
in the branches of my family tree.
How forlorn I have been
in the company of my kin,
where blood ceases to warm
my cold and hungry veins,
where I pray for the Gods to bring me
an answer to all the Mysteries
of my becoming.

Then you come like that happy little wren,
bearing my own countenance
from far beyond the shadow's greedy reach.
I tasted the foreign places I had hidden my heart,
by way of the song you carried,
with the Sun on your heaving breast.

Pitter-patter, pitter-patter!
This is the sound your heart makes in my ears,
weaving the near and the far
in a harmony that awakens me to the present.

O beloved,
I have brought you the very best I have,
the incense of my deeds,
by day and by night filled with desire,
the prostrations of my feet
upon the pilgrim's road.

You were like a temple to me,
whose gilt doors were fastened with silver bolts,
where day and night came together
to perform the dance of the ages.

Why have I wandered so far, coveted so much?
I was born from dissatisfaction,
having never accepted one sight
as the answer to all the Mysteries.

Your seed poured into me
from which a great tree grew.
It was like that World Tree
spoken of in the ancient songs and old fables,
its branches cascading down
until they met the raging sea.

A turtle braved these raging tides
to carry the world upon his back.
The Gods made a foothold within the impossible,
to carry forth their impossible dream.

Love is impossible,
and yet it happens
in the farthest reaches
of that cold and salty sea,
it finds a fjord
where the ragged cliffs cannot contain it.

From this impossible beginning
the Gods take the warp and the weft,
from which all is secreted together
in the bosom of the holy sea.

Holy sea, distant Mother
your crown is the Sun in the East
and the hallowed Moon in the West.
It is from their sacral light
that the blanket of Eternity is woven by the Gods,
They Who can never be eclipsed
as long as the world endures.

Upon that turtle's back
rode the Gods in the first beginning.
From Their loins did generations spring,
and I am one of those.

Your Mysteries poured into me,
like a pitcher of water.
I have found that I have no bottom,
no empty, no void and no cavern.
All have been filled with you, beloved,
as it was in the Ancient time.

The Gods Who filled the Earth have seen
and when we stop to take a drink
of the waters that surround us,
then we shall see all the things
that the Gods from the first beginning have seen.

6: Under the World Tree
The Beginning Before Beginnings

If you come here,
you come to the beginning.
Naked, stripped of all your worldly values,
you come here to the navel that existed,
before Moon became the sovereign
of the night sky;
before Sun uplifted the primordial mountains
from the formless abyss;
before were suspended the net of constellations,
kissing the veil with their timid lights;
before the Green God spewed His seed upon
the luxurious fields;
before came here the oceans, the cliffs,
the stony terraces of the land.

Written knowledge did not exist,
nor generations of philosophers
to give it a voice,
the Sky herself being without a voice,
the Earth in his puberty
without cognizance of his power.
But these are all the things
the World Tree remembers,
before there is thought and Gods and Spirits,
Ancestors and your kin.

So you come here naked,
when you come to seek the beginning
before the beginning.
You shed your skins,
one by one taking your heart
back to its conception,
tracing its life from branch to branch to branch.

Can you read your names inscribed in silver
against golden leaves,
illumined by the Sun in His morning awakening,
and gently tapped by the Moon,
when She unfurls Her alabaster sail
across the vault of lapis lazuli.
Constellations read you.
Stars proclaim your history.
The ears of the Gods converge in council
to decide your fate
amongst those billions of delicate stars.

In the green eternity of leaves is your fate
written as substantial as the ancient mountains,
whose fates are not known
even to the primordial Gods.

They came here too, in the beginning,
to see Their names written by starlight
upon these little leaves.
Their language having no sound familiar
to human ears.
Their meaning having no code of ethics,
no crime, no punishment, no prison
and no captives.

Before the will of humankind came into being,
there was no need for such shackles as these.
He clads himself in irons,
through a fate of his own design.
But it was not so in the beginning before beginnings,
beneath the World Tree.

Strip back your skins, O mortal soul!
Strip back your many ages,
when you come to the place before
your disguise was needed.
When the Gods and Their human kin settled
the Earth without separation between them.

Can you remember lapis sky
ensconced in the arms of malachite earth?
Can you still behold turquoise ocean
performing her dance,
over the crowns of highest mountains,
when from a net of stars,
the souls of humankind were chosen by the Gods?

This is where we had our beginning
before beginnings,
before the All were stripped down to the jealous one.
Do you not see through his clothes
anger, jealousy, rage, and annihilation?
In a bid for the throne of the world,
he swept the All away,
he felled the World Tree with a single swipe
of his jealous ax.

He tasted the blood of the world
while hailing to redeem it,
claiming victory through blood,
he has dressed the ages in skins of disguise.
Where is the Ancestral beginning?

Make quiet your language, your industry,
your contrived morality.
These things did not exist in the beginning,
before beginnings.
They were never inscribed upon the leaves
of the World Tree.

What you have inscribed with these things is death,
which came when your language came;
which came when your industry was forged;
which came when the fetters of your morality were woven,
to bind the thighs of mortals together.

Immortality exists under the World Tree,
where three roots pierce the ages;
where the memory of the beginning
before beginnings is kept;
where messages of the Ancient Times
have been secreted as treasures;
where the All had their births
before the one stole their skins;
before the disguises of mortals were conceived;
before the Earth shut away His mother
and exiled his sister;
before Her voices were forgotten
by living memory.

But you know where to find the immortality
of the beginning before beginnings.
For memory is our All, beyond the reach of one.
On our fingers we find a loom to count the days
back to our Ancient Time.
We find the answer in the language of numbers,
which takes us back before one existed.

Ply the heavenly vault for Her wisdom
and you shall find the answer there hidden,
written in the golden constellations,
which hail the All and leave the one to his shadows.
This is our true inheritance
from the beginning before beginnings.

If you come here,
you come to the beginning.
Naked, stripped of all your world's impositions,
you receive the inheritance of the All,
the Gods, the Spirits, the Ancestors and their kin.
These are the constellations dwelling
in the heaven of creation,
embraced by Memory,
beneath the roots of all the worlds.

These are the Truths that have existed
before the one was conceived.
These are the numberless leaves that grow
in the beginning before beginnings.

7: *Into the Mysteries*

Memory,
I keep vigil at your feet.
Having come with a lamp in my right hand,
I keep vigil at your feet.
With my left hand I hold the sacral earth,
wet and clad in shadows.
I hold onto the soil.
This is the place where I began.

Sky, my mother,
your constellations have found me
entering the bowels of the Earth.
A cave, shelter,
the stones in my ancient memory.
This is the place where we began.

Earth, my father,
your fields have awoken my verdant memory.
Where I was barren,
you have restored the heady scent of trees.
Cedar, ash, and yew,
I have their sap coursing through my veins.
This is the seed from which my life began.

Stillness,
I begin in the grave where all life begins.
We have come here before.
Yes we, for it is in ignorance that we
conceive of only one soul, when myriad
constellations burn with numberless stars.

Is there only one star, then?
One constellation?
One petal on a single flower?
One?
It cannot be, when nature has bequeathed us
such infinite variety,
when Her kisses are many,
and His seed speaks of multitudes.
This is where Creation began.

I feel my cloak fall from my bare shoulders,
the delicate light slide down my back
as a rivulet of molten gold.
A single light in the darkness,
where wait the Gods in silence
for my becoming.

My Mother waits for me
into the Mysteries.
My Father embraces me
into the Mysteries.
The light becomes shadow
into the Mysteries.
The empty spaces are abundance
into the Mysteries
The future is laid to rest
into the Mysteries.
The past becomes my rebirth
into the Mysteries.
Where silver transmutes into gold
into the Mysteries.
Where the Moon makes love to the Sun
into the Mysteries.
Where the elder becomes the babe
into the Mysteries.
Where the wise become the ignorant
into the Mysteries.
Where the hierophant becomes the neophyte
into the Mysteries.
Where the exalted becomes the initiate
into the Mysteries.
Where Father conceives me
into the Mysteries.
Where Mother seeds me
into the Mysteries.

I take up the torch as my guide,
the Gods are that guiding light.
I follow the pathway established before me,
these are the Ancestors who gave
their blood and bones before me.
Fear, you are my sustenance,
and joy, you are a promise waiting
silently in the future's dust.
This is the place where we all begin.

I call forth the God who dwells
in the Tree where the world began.
Let your green hand seed me,
your body become me.
Give me the dagger you grasp
in your strong right hand.
I receive its might,
and its myriad voices bestow unto me
the knowledge of all my Fathers.

I call forth the Goddess who dwells
in the sky which bore the Tree
where the world began.
Let your wet womb conceive me,
your blood become me.
Give me the light of the constellations
you hold in your thighs.
I receive their illumination
as a gateway to the Mysteries,
and these bestow unto me
the wisdom of all my Mothers.

My heart is my Mother.
My heart is my Mother.
My heart is my Mother of my many ages,
of my many lifetimes.
She births my Souls and gives speech to my names.
These are the seeds from where our lives begin.

Memories,
you find me in my sleep,
when I have lost the way before me,
my sight having forgotten
all the things it has seen before.
It is your heartbeat that startles me awake,
a drum that thunders in my ears,
a lightning that strikes my eyes
in the night.

This is where our rebirth begins,
into the Mysteries
where the ending begins,
and the beginning ends.

8: In the Sea of Beginnings

I behold a mount rising from the sea,
like that mount that rose in the first beginning.
Naked, without the embrace of the Sun,
without the grace of time or the ages,
of language or the industry of civilization,
I saw a mount rising from the eternally churning sea,
and even my wet heart knew
that this was how the first beginning began.

Our time and our industry has erased the Mother
of beginnings from our memory.
We have forgotten Her birth pangs,
Her coupling with Ancient Father;
Her gestation of the stars,
from which constellations came forth;
Her union with the Earth,
when She became the Sky;
Her dialogue with the ivory tongue of the Moon,
whose hallowed promise remains suspended
in the vault but for a timid moment;
Her anguish when Her children the stars
took their lights of life far from Her belly;
Her terror when the wind tore Ancient Father
from Her sacred embrace;
Her face when the brilliance of the Sun
shone out over the vault
as a mirror of molten and burnished gold,
when the Earth Himself was fructified, and all
living things were filled with the seed of life.

These are the miracles that came forth
from the womb of the Mother Sky,
who existed before the Sun existed.
He who became the Father of all fathers
was first mothered by Her primordial thighs.
And it is so that when a man is conceived
or couples with a woman,
he is reuniting his mortal body
with the immortal body of Mother.
And this is the ancient knowledge
that humankind has forgotten
in its descent into the industry
of the one.

Cold, naked,
my manhood hanging limp between my legs,
I behold a mount like a pyramid
rising from the sea,
the sea that has existed far beyond
the outer limits of our perception;
the hard and raging sea,
from which all that exists
has received the seed of its becoming;
the All from which the Many were given birth
in the Ancient Time.

Time, and time before time,
existed within Her womb,
within the body of the Ancient Mother-Father,
that cold and bottomless abyss
that so raged as to inspire the beginnings of the world,
its explosions and couplings,
its shooting seed and iridescent constellations.

I find that this is the abyss
where my cradle had its fashioning,
where my Mother and Father came together,
following after that ancient memory
spun by the first coupling of First Mother and First Father.
Theirs had been a coupling in the dark abyss of the All,
from which the Many were given birth
in the Ancient Time.

I find that we have inherited the Gods
without knowing it,
Their sacred trails blazing in the midnight sky,
Their prophecies spelled out
in the myriad constellations that share
the blue-black heavens with
the fragile reign of the Moon,
Their ancient power kept secret in the spires
of mountains that dominate every member
of Ancient Father's body,
Their names kept by the glaciers
and the high mountain lakes,
by azure waters placid and running,
Their true names, the secret knowledge of birds,
who possess the skies and alight
upon highest peaks.

And this is a language we have all but forgotten,
as the industry of the one has covered the Many
with a heavy blanket of shadows.
And his name is shadow,
and his shade is but one dark droplet,
which fell from the abyss of the All.

My thirst sees past this single droplet of shadow,
when I behold a mount rising from the sea,
that sea from which every droplet that has been born,
has found its beginning in the All
sea that cannot be one, and yet contains the Many.

Raging, surging, Their dance from the abyss
has fashioned the wet earth,
and brought its seed out of the darkness.
My seed, riding my thighs, swelling my member,
the power of my inheritance from Ancient Father.
What I grasp in my fist is the magic
through which generations were spun,
woven from the celestial fabric
of that abyss in blackness.

Black is the hallowed beginning;
black the abyss from whence the azure waters came;
black the abyss where the sapphire sky
met her embrace with wet earth;
black the womb where man has his entrance,
where the magic of beginnings
is secreted in the darkness.
And this is our inheritance
when we come out from the abyss
and into the light ruled by the Sun.
Crowned by mountains, the monarchs of East and West,
the earth we walk in daytime
has come out of the black,
its Mother and its Father,
our Mother and our Father.

Mother, I cannot forget you,
for I have inherited the sky from your womb.
Father, I cannot deny you,
for I have inherited the Earth from your body.
Sea, the ancient and surging,
the bottomless and without beginning,
the black and sacred abyss
where the constellations were born,
I come back to your embrace, to your wet magic,
to your fruit, to your knowledge forbidden.
I see, I taste, I touch, I smell.
I rekindle my Ancient memory woven by the Gods,
and I am triumphant, filled with wisdom, and reborn.

This is my inheritance now,
clothed in knowledge,
within the embrace of the Sun.
Having heard the ancient language,
having my years counted out before me,
having time dissolve in the presence
of my eternal soul.
I remember the Many droplets,
which fell from the All.
These whet my memory for the rest of my days,
while my nights give birth to wisdom
of what my two eyes have seen.

I behold a mount rising from the sea
like that mount that rose in the first beginning.

9: *Restoration of the Sacred*

Standing in darkness,
I stand where the first being stood,
the wind gnawing at my back,
while the empty landscape howls
through my heart.
Where is the comfort of language,
existing in the beginning, and
somehow lost by the wayside
as the journey unfolded?

I draw up my knees
on the cold earth
my hands, my fingers, my skin
and my blood.
My bones too are of this Earth,
and I draw them up in silence,
for all language has deserted me,
as it deserted the first being
who became as a child
upon the nourishing soil
where I now lay.

My burial shroud is the skin of the Earth,
its soil the umbilical cord that feeds me;
its damp cavern, the amniotic sack that envelops me,
the heady fragrance of its flowers,
the incense that invokes my name to rise;
its streams my mother's tears,
when she fought to deliver me;
its peaks the loins of my father,
from which my manhood arose;
its fire my blood, heating my veins,
as Winter's breath draws near;
its wind the stirring of my lungs,
when Summer chases the shade with molten light;
its blessings and its curses become me,
as I come from its gap,
this Earth of mine, standing now
where the first being stood.

What language does the Earth speak
before the ego of man claims it?
The whispering stream, the rushing wind,
the tumbling mountains,
these are the words of Ancient Father,
who once gazed up at Mother Sky in admiration,
urging his loins to thrust upwards to meet her.

The dance they did
caused the constellations to spray forth,
to illumine the hungry darkness
where no being stood.
I light a torch for Ancient Father and Mother Sky.

Ancient Father, you are the mound of the beginning
that divided the churning sea.
Your light became the kernel of life in the angry depths.
The surging ocean,
without bottom and without direction,
became your inspiration in the dark.

Darkness, she is the seed of all life where he bursts,
where darkness becomes the fluid of life inside her.
I awaken the darkness of life with the burst of my fire,
O Ancient Father, whose workings are
the names from which creation springs.
I alight upon your darkness,
here in the place where the first being stood.

Mother Sky, I carry a light for you
as you have carried lights for me.
The infinite constellations whose fires
have burned for millions upon millions of years,
these have shined from before the beginning of beings,
illumining the way,
though the eyes of humankind
are often veiled against their knowledge.

Knowledge, she is the flower whose nectar has fed
the universe from its dark beginning.
She is the legacy of all beings who labor for her,
though she turns away her face from those
who squander what they have been given.

O Ancient Father and Mother Sky,
I summon the knowledge you have woven,
through the warp of darkness and the weft of light;
warp of womb and weft of seed;
warp of knowledge and weft of labor;
warp of conscience and weft of action;
warp of mind and weft of hands;
warp of heart and weft of intellect;
warp of inspiration and weft of industry;
warp of Spirit and weft of body;
warp of Soul and weft of flesh.
These all are the workings of your sacred bodies,
from which the existence of all things has been fashioned.
This is the knowledge of the First Gods,
your Gods,
you people who stand where I now stand
here in the place where the first being stood.

When you light a torch from the air
that surrounds you,
when you inject light into the dark places
you have been given,
these are the gifts of the immortal Gods,
whose language cannot be separated
from the air drawn in by the lungs.
As long as mortals have lungs,
and as long as lungs may draw in the air,
there shall be language,
and the Gods who dwell therein.

We do not go forth in silence, my body and this Spirit of mine
we move through the warp and the weft
the Gods have woven from the beginning of time.
It is inseparable from our condition yes, 'we',
for there is no longer an 'I' in my sacred condition.
We are the life the providence of the Gods
has ordered in the darkness,
where light becomes the weft
to the warp of the dark beginning.

We returned there, to that darkness,
to stand where the first being stood,
the wind gnawing at our back,
while the empty landscape howled through our heart.

The comfort of language is now with us again,
as long as the mind remembers that it was here,
here in this dark place,
where all life in the Gods began,
here in the Earth,
where the first being stood.

10: In the Womb of the Hidden Chamber

We have come to the Hidden Chamber,
which dwells in the nether regions of the ancient Earth,
His bowels which have always existed
beneath our mortal feet, drawing them down.
His soil has kept me fed
with the knowledge of the Gods.
It ripens on the Great Tree,
glistens in the indestructible Sun,
which I take to my breast.

I behold the clouds that pass through Mother Sky
as She reaches down to embrace Him.
What She bestows in the Sun's radiance,
is the coming again of life to the world,
which never ceases in its cycles
nor tires in its seasons.

She reaches down to Him,
and, with the tips of Her sacred fingers,
She blesses Him with the power of Her seed,
the seed from which the Great Tree grew,
bore fruit, bursting forth as the kernel
of the eternal Sun.

How he shines for the Mother who begat him.
How he shines for the Earth who receives him.
How he returns from the dark cavern of
the twilight sky which swallows him.
How he hails the rosy gold dawn,
which splits the heavens for him.
How he carries the stars which salute
the holy light which clothes him.
How he wears the circumpolar stars upon
his never setting brow which crowns him.
How he tastes the waters below,
and brings with him the celestial flood
upon which the dead travel,
these secret things passing in and out with him
upon the bosom of the sacred sky.

Have you not heard the crashing of the dawn
upon the ancient mountains of the world?
It is the morning tide,
when the Great Goddess removes, one by one,
the scintillating veils of the night sky,
Her lover from the twilight hour
having painted her body with constellations,
the circumpolar stars his kisses,
the Milky Way his ecstasy,
surging through Her golden thighs.

My ears were awakened
with such an eruption of music,
that even in my grave I found sleep impossible.
The Earth about me cannot deafen His ears
to the stirring of that Great Goddess,
who stretches out Her body across
the vault of the indigo sky.

Painted with light for Her, the Sun himself kisses
her navel as he passes through her legs
in celebration of the holy dawn.
Its music is the joy of the ages expressed all at once,
the dead bursting through the crust of the Earth
from their cradles in the Netherworld.
Their music, at once terrible and beautiful,
pricks the drums of my ears,
while the drum of my heart beats freely again.

Come music, let me hear you again!
Come love, let me make you again!
Come dawn, let me drink your light again!
Come sky, let me pass through your gleaming thighs again!
Come stars, circumpolar and eternal,
bursting with life within the darkness of the sapphire veil,
let my two eyes carry your light again!
Come Earth, let my feet be firmly planted in your soil again!
Come mountains, east and west,
the two horizons from which birth and rebirth are sent forth,
let me pass between you again,
through you and charged with your sacral powers again!
Come dawn and twilight, find me in my lover's arms again!

There is nothing that awaits us in the beyond
that can surpass the fragile beauty
of drawing breath upon the Earth,
seeing the Sun rise over the eastern mountains of the world,
beholding with our two eyes the most delicate blue
spreading with pink ribbons across the effervescent ocean,
drawing air into the lungs,
and drinking life while the heart dances.

This is the dance we have come for,
from the cradle to the grave.
This is what we were fashioned for,
and for no other purpose have we been conceived
than to live,
which is a higher purpose
than any prophet can foretell or wise man proclaim.

Life is the only beginning we have,
which the Gods prepare in the womb of the Hidden Chamber.
It births the Soul as it births the dying Sun,
to send out its light once more
into the hungry darkness.

Before I die and before I am reborn,
I reach down into my heart
to find all the stones that I have carried with me
through my many ages,
the stones that have weighed me down,
one by one,
and made my heart too heavy to carry.
The Gods with their two all-seeing eyes
stare out from beyond the veil,
and they watch my hands cast them out.

Regret, you are a stone, and I cast you out.
Selfishness, you are a stone, and I cast you out.
Guile, you are a stone, and I cast you out.
Jealousy, you are a stone, and I cast you out.
Hatred, you are a stone, and I cast you out.
Exclusion, you are a stone, and I cast you out.
Anger, you are a stone, and I cast you out.
Suffering, you are a stone, and I cast you out.
Sorrow, you are a stone, and I cast you out.
Loneliness, you are a stone, and I cast you out.
Ignorance, you are a stone, and I cast you out.
Death, you are a stone, and I cast you out.

What I find on the tips of my fingers
are the lights of stars, shining with abandon
in the lapis sphere above my head.
These are joy and pleasure,
love and sacred friendship.
They come as knowledge coupled with wisdom,
which sprout as the leaves
decorating the Great Tree with life.

Have you never seen the leaves of the Great Tree,
rooted to the hallows of the ancient Earth
in the womb of the Hidden Chamber?
This is where the Gods come,
it is where we come from,
when we come from that place we call
the darkness of our beginnings,
when we come back into the life
that has returned from the Hidden Chamber.

11: Lighthouses of Memory

What must a man do to recapture his memory?
Silence is the answer my heart gives,
while the past nods in satisfaction,
it knows that all souls must embrace it
like a lover, and cling to its breast
as to our mother's own.

Future, I do not comprehend your names
or have sight of your spectral forms.
You are a mystery to my intelligence.
The present, you are lonely and confused to me,
for you lack memory of your beginnings.
But where shall I find you, if not in the past,
where Mother's breast fed me Her heavenly milk,
and Father's body fed me His terrestrial seed?

As a child I was told that there are two lighthouses
in the harbor of time,
whose beacons are called present and future.
Their lights wink and glitter like the bodies of stars,
in which mortals wander to satisfy their appetites.
They say that the future is bright,
without ever having met him.
And they say that the present is all we truly have,
without ever having asked him his purpose.

But when I came into the harbor as a boy,
I saw a third lighthouse shimmering
like a great bonfire,
its foundation an ancient precipice stretching
far into the mist.

Her name was Past,
and she was the wife of the future
and the mistress of present.
She had other names about her,
which I could see spelled out
in the stony steps of that precipice;
memory, recognition, and restoration were with her.

I remembered her children;
magpie, crow, and gull,
whose furious and constant chattering
filled the innumerable pages
of dusty volumes I had collected.

Others warned me of magpie.
He gathered in his little beak
all trivial and useless things discarded by the rest.
Crow, he fed off the triumphs of others,
picking apart the fruits of their labors,
like an unwanted house guest.
And gull, his companion over the cold and restless sea,
was a scavenger after the miseries deposited on the waves,
left to the tides.

I found that magpie, crow, and gull were useful to me.
Flying between past and present,
they brought back with them the markings
of a nest I recognized as future's hidden gift.
While others saw the discarded, jaded, and useless,
I saw the makings of my own nest.
My heart read their attributes and saw
remembrance, roots, and longevity.

But an old sea captain came out
from a collapsing vessel called anger,
whose anchor was called jealousy.
He raged with his white and ancient beard,
proclaiming the existence of a single lighthouse.
"There is only one,"
his violent eyes and flared nostrils said to me,
"there is only one!"

Only one?
One source of light and one beacon to carry it?
One lighthouse for safety, and one flame in its hearth
to restore a place called home?
One star in the night sky,
which shelters but a single constellation?
One breath of wind and one droplet of condensation?
One bird upon the wind and one wing to cut the single air?
One breath left in my lungs, and only one life left to live?

What a fool!
My heart, counting its many breaths and many beats,
recognized the drum of myriads from which all life thunders.
We came from that ancient and restless sea called history,
whose secret name is memory.
My ship, my guide, and the harbor my heart comes home to.
The light of your bonfire is cast between present and future,
you are the fuel of present and succor of the future,
from which my heart draws its future rebirths.
Your secret name belies the jealousy of one,
who ever only sees himself,
and knows his own terrible solitude.
There is no future with him
for the liberated flight of my soul.

My soul, his name is heron
who flies with sparrow and swallow
over the ancient and restless sea.
Darkness is his kin, who fed him the light in solitude.
Light is the air that stirs his wings,
the shade that spreads out before his dancing feet.
Shade is his illumination, which shows him the sacred way.
Wind is his memory,
which flows from south to north, east to west,
taking with it the flight of souls
returning to their nests in Eternity.

Above my head shine the myriad constellations
in their fathomless courses in the vault.
Their histories dispel the jealousy of one
to have all and be all.
For the All cannot be comprehended,
nor can it be contained or enumerated by the one.
One cannot erase the immortality of memory,
passed down by a mother through the milk
of her hidden history,
history passed down through the very skin
of the Earth, and the seas which cradle it.

We shall all come back to our beginning
in the end when breath begins to fail us,
when eyesight escapes us.
For there are other breaths and other eyes
of sight to be seen.
These are the eyes, the sights, the breaths
that we have all taken before,
and they travel with us down
through our Mother's milk.
Our Father's seed contains it, our Mother's
womb safeguards it.
And it is our future to return to our past,
where we received it in secret.

Magpie brought me this secret,
near the ancient and restless sea.
What others had discarded,
he brought back home to me.
A prophecy of the heart,
whose beats thunder as a drum,
a voice whose memory speaks of many,
stretching back before the one.

12: Sol Invictus
Return of the Light

Gap in the Earth,
from which the daytime sky wanders far,
becomes the companion of man
at the moment of his initiation.
Like that passage from which he emerged as a babe,
this secret Mother holds him close
to the Mystery of his beginning.
Where is sky and where are stars,
whose spectral lights haunt the globe of the Moon?
She pulls a milky veil through the midnight sky
to clothe its nakedness before Earth's ravenous gaze.

I came here as a man, naked and alone,
but not forlorn in the presence of the cavern
of the sky beneath the Earth,
this gap of hallows where the dead return to sup
from the passage of the midnight sun.
And I have seen the ghostly flesh of the Sun,
float fast upon the waters of the river
which splits the ancient Earth.
This river of hallows, where the lonely dead hail,
the brief and glittering course of light blazed
through the Underworld by Grandfather Sun.

Constellations and your divine entourage,
I seek your whirling dance,
in the cavern beneath the Earth.
Champion who wields the sacrificial knife,
his tall cap wreathed in celestial light.
O Bull, grappled and trussed, whose bright red blood
feeds the denizens of the Underworld.
Scorpion who seizes the fecund spoils of the Bull.
Raven, black sovereign of the sky beneath the Earth,
who takes his throne upon the flank of sacral Bull.
O Bull, whitest of all the hallows,
whose blood nourishes the living and the dead,
whose haunches meet the Earth
but whose nostrils pierce the heavens.
O Dog and Snake, gorged upon the blood of the Bull,
you three ears of golden wheat born from Bull's gore,
you torch-bearers, whose sacred fires illuminate the way,
a torch pointed to the vault and one to the Earth below.
I come to the place where your Mysteries are spelled out,
within the bowels where the dead are swallowed whole,
and where the dead are given the boon of eternal life.

O Sun beneath the Earth, Sol Invictus,
I stand naked beneath your wheel in the midnight sky,
where blankets of light proclaim Luna who found me,
where molten fire renews my flesh by Sol's sovereign power.

For all people come to this place,
where the dead fear their own shadows,
where they wait for the hope of the Sun to be reborn,
here in the celestial hall of Ancient Earth's body,
the destiny of every soul
 who has passed through the belly of a mother.

Is it our destiny, then, to be alone and in darkness
at the end, as we were in the beginning?
When we come to the gap in the world,
there shall be no companion;
no clothing or fortune;
no rank or humility;
no possession or poverty;
no dominance or cowardice;
no debate or eloquence;
no gender or identity;
no flesh or manhood;
no will or womb;
no suffering or ecstasy;
no gluttony or denial.
For these are the disguises we adopt,
when we take the road of the world
that stretches out after our mother's womb.
She cannot find us again,
when we are alone at the gap of the world
that finds us in the end.

Initiation,
I have found you in each of the forms I have taken
in each of the ages of my life,
when I change my bodies like I change my clothes.
I carry on the inside
what cannot be carried over on the outside,
and these are the only treasures
I may carry in my empty arms,
when I arrive at that gap in the world
where the Sun does not shine.

Find my spirit, O Mother of the sky,
and shine on me as you shine
upon that raven whose black feathers ride you.
Find my body, O Father of the Earth,
and renew my skin as you renew
the faces of mountains and their kin,
these things that change from age to age,
and yet in their essence remain true.

Let me drink the azure sky as a spirit,
for Spirit has no thirst
for the ephemeral things of the Earth.
But while I am still made of flesh, made of earth,
let me drink of Spirit,
for flesh that drinks of Spirit while it is still flesh
shall drink true life and will know immortality.

Am I ever alone then,
when I come to the gap in the world at the end?
Are we alone in death and in our passage
from age to age to age?
We follow Grandfather Sun
as his ancient skin slips through the crack in the West,
where wait for him the legions of spirits,
who have all passed down before him.

They do not whisper, but shout
as his gilded countenance cuts the heavy darkness to ribbons,
his voice cascading down like music carried aloft
on a spring morning.
All the constellations find him,
their embrace removes the midnight veil
through which he has passed,
through which we shall pass.
Thus we cannot be alone, nor have we ever been alone,
nor has any living creature been alone,
when they come to the gap in the world.

For this I dance in the sky,
when its patterns fall across the shadow of the Earth,
the constellations having foretold our ages,
many ages ago,
our lifetimes reflected in Heaven's burnished silver mirror.
I fear neither shadow nor death,
for the seeds of light and life live in these things,
shadow being only the play of light upon form,
and death being the removal of life to another form.

It is with gratitude that I have imbibed this knowing,
and received the fast and flowing blood of the Mysteries
in my two outstretched palms.
Only the Gods bestowing such boons to those
whose hearts have been cracked open wide.

Sol Invictus is my name,
when I reappear from that gap in the world,
where earth and sky, life and death,
are meted out and divided.
I have reappeared upon my horizon,
where all life reappears;
where the dead reappear;
where the dawn sky reappears;
where the morning star reappears;
where the body of the Sun reappears;
where Spring reappears;
where the verdant earth reappears;
where youth reappears;
where all the things we have lost reappear,
after they have been swallowed by that gap in the world.

Take my dance, take my many ages,
and take my many faces down with you into the abyss.
Remember where you came from,
that gap in the Earth, where all that exists,
all that has ever existed, and all that shall ever exist,
has come forth like the face of the Sun.

13: Enter the Labyrinth
What Yew Tree Gave Me

I remember a giant yew tree,
stretching out to tangle
the night sky in its branches,
branches that held the messages of Gods
and spirits wandering the Earth.
Hungry yew tree to receive the voices and languages
of generations dead and as yet unborn.
Hungry yew tree, to receive the passage of the ages,
in remembrance of all that has happened,
and as yet unknown.
Unknown too are the future courses of stars yet unborn.
But Yew Tree knows these,
and is hungry to tell.

I passed by Yew Tree on my way to the labyrinth,
with myrtle at my brow and acorn about my heart.
I carry with me the insignia of the Gods below,
they who have tasted every life, every death,
and every piece of living fabric in the universe.
My eyes behold their otherworldly lights,
flickering on the distant horizon,
red for blood, knowing the beginning;
green for flesh, knowing the passions of form;
azure for spirit, passing between the worlds;
yellow for immortal memory, which transcends
flesh and form, death and impermanence;
and white for the Gods, having existed before the beginning,
and traveling beyond the end.

My insignia is the green and the red,
having received the boons of myrtle and acorn,
which belong to those senses, kept warm between my thighs,
the blood of my Mother and the seed of my Father,
who travel fast with me into the labyrinth.
Within my veins I carry them, all who have gone before,
within my bones I marry them,
whose memories provide the door.

Sacred drums beat while I shiver beneath
constellations traversing the body of the Veiled One.
She dances, casts off the burnished glare of the day,
taking the Moon as Her crown to set the world at its rest.
I hail Her with my body,
my naked feet firm planted in the black earth.
Black, the inheritance of new souls
drinking life within the womb.
Black, the inheritance of the dead
drinking the Mysteries in the end we meet,
more secret than our first beginning.

Where do I travel in labyrinth's holy keep?
North, where hails the wind cutting through the Earth.
South, where hails the water cutting through stone.
East, where hails the Sun whose light cuts through all.
West, where hails the Earth into which the Sun falls.

Into darkness, beyond music and passions and succor,
I carry the badges of the Gods upon my breast,
my heart being the keepsake of all my ages,
of my many lives within this life.
Yew tree has spoken to me of myriad leaves and branches,
each bearing a name and a bundle of years,
tied together with a thread knotted
by the Goddess of weaving,
these all are enumerated and known by the Primordials,
who existed before the First Beginning.

What say my leaves and my bundle,
my thread and the knots that tie them?
Do they speak of tender nights, the Moon clasped
firm in my naked fingers, the stars my lovers,
the Milky Way my climax?
Or do they speak of loves lost, regret and his minions,
left as stains and scents of cologne
upon discarded bedclothes?
Do they tell of Sun's twilight visits to warm the blood
in my anxious veins?
And what of memory, deep-seated, and passed down
by my Mother, when she gave me her generous breast?

I remember giant Yew Tree
who spoke to me as a child.
He told me about suffering, loss, and emptiness
like Sky that waits for Earth
beyond the reach of Sun's jealous hands.
"I would live," he said,
"only to die and then to be born again.
These are the Mysteries whose knots can never be unraveled,
though they can be known.
Knowing is memory, and memory is accounting
of all that has come before
and such memory is in the keeping of the Gods,
whom the jealous god has sought to suppress."
But Yew Tree came before the jealous god,
its golden branches and malachite leaves
being host to myriad constellations, to the myriad Gods,
these Primordials hosted by the Veil whose fabric
the jealous god may not tear.

"All of the Gods that ever were and ever shall be
have found their birth in me,"
said Yew Tree to the ears of my heart,
which still bore wetness behind them.
And Yew Tree spoke out the names
of the Primordial Gods to me.
When he had finished, my boyhood was gone,
and my adolescence had come.

Having found an altar within the labyrinth,
I placed what I had in sacrifice to the Gods of memory
- myrtle, which spoke of love and youth and desire,
when it crackled upon the fire,
and golden acorns of Earth's heavenly tree,
which spoke of Ancient Father's power
swimming inside me.

To give up what is precious may seem like folly
in the eyes of the outer world,
where wealth is power and power is a vise's hold
upon the lives of others.
But to give freely, even as the Sun gives,
is to receive love that outlasts the shadow of mortality,
knowing and memory, which can be carried beyond
the shadow of the mortal form.

Passing from form to form to form
is the memory which Yew Tree gave me,
memory which the jealous god, who is only one,
can never possess.
Thus he has forbidden its knowledge to all of humankind.
The Primordial Gods who came before him,
are the keepers of memory,
memory of every form through which every being
has passed and shall pass.
Is our memory the knowledge that even he shall pass,
and is that why such knowledge is forbidden?

Yew Tree heard the beating of my heart
secreted within the labyrinth.
All hearts are naked here, spilling their secrets
like the river at flood time.
What did Yew Tree whisper to me
from the four corners of the ancient stones,
existing from the beginning of humankind?

From North you have the gift of breath,
from which flows the inheritance of speech.
From South you have the gift of blood,
from which flows the inheritance of regeneration.
From East you have the gift of intelligence,
from which flows the inheritance of memory.
And from West you have the gift of form,
from which flows the gift of existence.
These are the gifts the Primordial Gods
have given to humankind.
Without them, humankind would cease to exist,
and existence is what Yew Tree has witnessed,
from the time of the First Beginning.

I don the smoke of myrtle and acorn
upon my naked skin
I stand beneath the sky clad only in sky
I stand firm in the earth,
with the Earth as my witness.
I tap the earth with my naked fingers,
carrying nothing and grasping for nothing.
Whatever is given me is not mine as my possession,
it is only a gift that passes through me,
taking with it the memory of my existence.
And this is the fruit which fell
from the Tree of Knowledge which Yew Tree knows,
what I know now after entering the labyrinth
woven by the Gods.

My naked face houses naked eyes,
clad only in knowing and in memory.
Knowing my names and my forms,
as branches and leaves and knots
in Yew Tree's keeping.
I dance as the clouds dance,
as the sky dances;
as the constellations, kindred of the sky dance;
as the moon, lover of the youthful sun dances;
as the Milky Way, climax of the Universe dances;
as the ancient earth, prodigious of cave
and mountain dances;
as the tempestuous sea dances;
as the colors of twilight dance;
as the dew of morning's awakening dances;
as life and death dance together beneath,
the primordial branches of Yew Tree who dances.

When I am old at heart and can no longer dance,
I shall come back to the labyrinth,
which Yew Tree has sheltered since the time
of humankind's beginning,
where I first heard his voice falling from
the naked sky at dawn.
Clad only in the sky,
I shall enter the labyrinth's winding memory
where memory of me shall linger
until the very last being has nothing left
to remember.

14: Navel
Return of the Gods

Where has our memory gone,
and where did we lose it?
Is it like a stone
one finds on a lonely beach,
casting it into the hungry tide
to be devoured by time?
Is it instead the delicate light
of Moon in her waxing,
cherishing the sapphire sky
in the company of stars,
burning then burning out?
Is it like love itself,
stronger still only in the moments
after it is lost?
Does one ever find it again?

I have found my cloak
beneath that acorn tree I saw
painted strongly against a pale blue sky,
its branches spread out far above
my unclad toes, making hallowed the wind
that kissed it as it breathed the sacred names.
Name, sound, language and memory
I find you locked away where I have cast you,
not of my own accord.
When I was born I did not know I had these,
hurled away deep in that stronghold and guarded
by the jealous god.
Should I have wrestled him to gain back my memory?

Cloak to my shoulders, sky to my thighs,
I am a journeyer after that sacred stone
my memory had thrown away when I was born.
As I traversed the stony road,
scattered with broken leaves,
I remember my mother telling me
the tale of a garden once inhabited
by man in his youth,
its luxuriant beauty a home where the body
could remain sky-clad, where the memory too
was verdant and evergreen.

The Tree of Knowledge burst through the black earth,
gathering the clouds and counting them with language,
language not yet forbidden by the jealous god,
who guarded the tree with suspicion day and night.

It was sky-clad heroine, forerunner of the race of humans,
who took the fruit of the tree and ate it,
handing it down to ravenous man
whose longing for knowledge
exceeded his ability to use it.
Crestfallen heroine, together with her kin which sprang from
her loins, was banished from the garden by the jealous god,
who ever after forbade
the gathering of fruit from this garden,
and felled the Tree of Knowledge where it had stood
since the dawn of the world.

And that is how memory and most ancient language
were lost to the god called anger and jealousy,
who possessed the heavens and the Earth but desired
to eat every mortal heart.

That is how humankind was born
without memory and language,
excepting those hearts whose nourishment had been
so strong as to provoke the distant sounds of memory,
beating stronger still than a human heart is wont to beat.

Has mine always beaten so strong?
Strong against the jealous wind, beating;
strong against the persistent tides, beating;
strong against the unshakable mountains, beating;
strong against the hungry twilight sky, beating;
strong against stones with names like commandment,
judgment, and wrathful, beating;
strong with the distant and fragile language of memory,
its notes and phrases having haunted the forlorn caverns
of my heart since before I was born.

"There is a place secreted away at the top of a mountain,"
Giant Oak Tree said to me,
"and its center is the navel of the world,
where two golden eagles met.
Hallowed earth and molten crown of sky it bears,
their names are known as language and memory.
This is the place where the sovereign of the sky
sent his powers,
where people would find the voice of the ages,
waiting patiently beneath the blanket of silence
woven by the jealous god."

Thus I climbed,
higher still than the other forbidding mountains,
their crests haloed with electric clouds,
with names like forgetfulness, pacify, and fear.
Why was I not afraid, when my memory conjured
the bliss of ignorance, the fullness of satisfaction,
and the constancy of being afraid?
But stronger still was my thirst for language
and my hunger for the sounds of memory.

"Have you ever caught the sound of memory
ringing deep in the ears of your heart?
Have you ever been called, when you are abandoned,
deep down within that cavern of forgetfulness
called home again by the distant powers
of the ancient heart, still beating, beating?"

This is what I heard over the tops
of those angry and jealous clouds,
gnawing at my insides
like the talon of a disgruntled bird of prey.
My thirst was too strong for fear.
My hunger too great an adversary
for forgetfulness to work its way in
and gain a permanent foothold.
I saw the storm clouds gathering,
and my heart said let them pass on by.

Mountain calling,
with a voice unmistakable as Ancient Memory,
fruit of the Tree of Knowledge, felled but not forgotten.
I gathered up its branches in my winnowing arms,
my tender fingers plucking them up like strings
of a harp played only by the whispers of the wind.
Putting back each note in place,
caressing each leaf until it unfurled,
I found my way back to the navel
where two golden eagles once met.
Is this where the Tree of Knowledge once stood,
golden and unencumbered against the winter sky?

I found its stony trunk,
firm planted in the rocky black earth.
Waiting patiently throughout the ages,
it hungered for the sounds of memory
known only to the sparrows,
who dipped and darted over the forgotten landscape.
Have I remembered the language in their keeping,
the Ancient Memory guarded jealously by all the ages?

Enter, my voice, strong and undiluted,
to recite the litany woven
before the jealous god stole his throne
of unassailable victory.
Unassailable, but for the language of Ancient Memory,
which once hung ripe from the Tree of Knowledge,
more fearful to him than the sound
of unbreakable silence is to our ears.

But I saw the Navel Stone standing firm
where the Tree of Knowledge once stood
and gathering my voice,
greater still than a winter thunderstorm,
I recited the litany,
in whose language Ancient Memory had waited.

"Gods of the Sky,
Her body the Mother of the never-setting stars,
I throw open the doors of the sky,
I open the doors that were closed!

"Gods of the Imperishable Stars,
the Indestructibles and their kin,
I throw open the doors of the stars,
I open the doors that were closed!

"Gods of the Clouds,
riding high and undefeated over the indigo vault,
I throw open the doors of the clouds,
I open the doors that were closed!

"Gods of the Sun,
whose strength endures as the cycles of the Sun endure,
I throw open the doors of the Sun,
I open the doors that were closed!

"Gods of the Moon,
striking love in the tides and the hearts of humankind,
I throw open the doors of the moon,
I open the doors that were closed!

"Gods of the Earth,
fecund, yielding, pregnant with memory,
I throw open the doors of the Earth,
I open the doors that were closed!

"Gods of the Mountains,
ancient, unmovable, cutting the sky with stony spires,
I throw open the doors of the mountains,
I open the doors that were closed!

"Gods of the Seas,
primordial and ever-nascent
with the knowledge of beginnings,
I throw open the doors of the seas,
I open the doors that were closed!

"Gods of the Rivers,
bleeding from the ancient Earth and coupled with the seas,
I throw open the doors of the rivers,
I open the doors that were closed!

"Gods of the Heights,
from whose aspirations all souls had their birth,
I throw open the doors of the heights,
I open the doors that were closed!

"Gods of the Depths,
from whose primordial bodies the flesh
of all living creatures emerged,
I throw open the doors of the depths,
I open the doors that were closed!

"Gods of the North,
source of the cogent wind,
I throw open the doors of the North,
I open the doors that were closed!

"Gods of the South,
source of the flood of beginnings,
I throw open the doors of the South,
I open the doors that were closed!

"Gods of the East,
source of invigorating sun and its fire,
I throw open the doors of the east,
I open the doors that were closed!

"Gods of the West,
source of the gap in the Earth
where all souls are swallowed and live again,
I throw open the doors of the West,
I open the doors that were closed!

"Gods of Air,
I throw open the doors of the spirit,
I open the doors that were closed!

"Gods of Water,
I throw open the doors of the flesh,
I open the doors that were closed!

"Gods of Fire,
I throw open the doors of consciousness,
I open the doors that were closed!

"Gods of Earth,
I throw open the doors of immortality,
I open the doors that were closed!

"Ancestors of Light,
dwelling in the bones of the Earth,
I call you up from the darkness,
and throw open the doors of your ancestral memory,
I open the doors that were closed!"

Clad only in the sky, clad only in the lamps of stars,
I pass back into the Ancient Memory,
from which the Tree of Knowledge sprung its roots,
these reaching through the bowels of the Earth,
to touch the face of the sky on the other side.
I call its names, I provoke its memories,
and with my finger's tips I touch its navel.

Has our memory ever gone,
and did we ever lose it?
Isn't it like a stone we gather
on a lonely beach,
to be salvaged from the hungry tide,
to inspire the ages of time?
Isn't it instead a powerful light,
cutting through the forgetfulness of nightfall?
Isn't it rather like a star,
whose distant radiance travels
millions of millions of miles from its source,
shining, then shining again?
Or is it rather like love itself,
stronger after we lose it,
then find it waiting again?

15: Heart
Pilgrimage to the Gods

"Why should I bow,"
your heart says to me,
"when, firmly rooted to the Earth,
my feet walk of their own accord?
The road ahead being mine.
The destination being mine.
The volition being mine.
The eyes being mine.
The sight being mine.
The senses and their organs,
being all mine.
Why should my feet scrape,
and why should my heart
be subservient to their will?"

These are the challenges
your heart offers to me,
when I, in my dazzling white cloak,
make ready to move my feet
to the sound of the pilgrim's drum.

It beats beneath the sky
in a rhythm my ears have remembered
from ages long since passed over
by the anxious clouds.
How progress has claimed us,
while the heart grows famished
for consolation of the spirit.

"Do I bow,"
my heart says back to you,
"or is it the Earth beneath my feet,
that bows while the sky rises higher,
and the two horizons claim their prize
of heaven's flame?

"This is where I have warmed my empty veins
after death claimed me,
and what you see before your eyes
is a body of light moving fast,
over the charnel ground where earth and flame
have met my mortal flesh."

"Does the Earth bow,"
the lips of my heart say to you,
"or is it the Sky that bows when twilight claims her?
She gazes with her celestial lenses,
the noble ascent of the Moon to her throne,
while the tides follow after her
with a lover's urgent fingers.

"Do the stars bow to an empty sky,
filling with light a tranquil mirror
of the sea raging below?
Do their gilt arms reach with devotion
to the sphere of the Earth beneath them
or is it the constellations that truly reign,
dictating the courses of the world
to follow in their entourage?"

Now I am following after them,
these silver and spectral lights.
Flashing in a dark veil above my head,
my brow absorbs their direction,
pouring down not as water,
but as knowledge composed of light.

"Do I bow,"
my heart's eyes say to you,
"or do my eyes gaze upward
while my knees meet the Earth
in sacred congress?
This is how the Earth and Sky dance
how flesh mingles with Spirit
as Ether whirls through them.

"This is what all the sages have come to teach us,
they having been born of the flesh,
yet united with the Spirit.
It is Spirit that moves their feet,
to walk the soil where
the luster of stars has been concealed.
And this is what the Ancients left
in the wake of their well-traveled feet.

"The burden of proof gleams
above your head and below your feet.
For there exist not only stars
moving through the roof of the world,
but also those that change their courses
beneath the hallowed ground,
where caverns drink rivers unseen by human eyes."

I travel there,
not only with my ghostly feet,
but with the grateful movements of my heart.
Its blood carries my life from the center
to the outer reaches of my fingers.
"And does my heart bow,"
it asks you in your disbelieving stupor,
"or does it follow its natural design,
carrying out the life that flows into it,
as I move with the cadence its beating prescribes?"

I look to the Earth,
and see the trees in the wind bow.
I look to the Sky,
and see the stars of the veil bow.
I look to the clouds,
and see the birds on the air bow.
I look to the mountains,
and see the fire of the Sun bow.
I look to the night,
and see the darkness of the vault bow.
I look to twilight,
and see the authority of the Sun bow.
I look to life,
and see the certainty of breath bow.
And at last I look to Death,
and see the certainty of endings bow.

I need no consolation
when my end comes,
when my pilgrimage reaches its destination,
its two feet having exhausted every mortal possibility.
The ears of my heart have heard the cadence of stars,
those above and those below.
The eyes of my heart have seen knowledge of stellar courses,
in which is hidden what I know.

16: Spirit
Memory of the Gods

I arrived,
where at long last I am kissed by the Sun
in the moment of his triumph over the shadows.
I have seen with my own two eyes
the sphere of the Earth,
its illuminated horizon reaching, stretching,
tying a string to my heart with gilded thread.

This Sun, this Sky, this Earth
are bodies bound to mine;
as my mother is bound to me;
as my father is bound to me;
as I have eaten a ripe fruit,
from the Tree of Knowledge;
as I have felled shadow when it has fallen;
as I have swam in darkness,
while treading water to the light.

I have never been captured
in snares, nets or brambles set against me.
These adversaries called obedience, fear, and mediocrity,
they were never able to contain my heart,
which burst into flame at the breast of a sparrow,
being carried higher, ever higher
into the limitless veil.

What I have seen
with my two eyes
are sparrows weighed down with plummets,
their heads and delicate wings turned down
to the covetous Earth,
whose gravity placed upon them
weights hailed as tradition, duty, and law,
these things that bend free wing and feather
to their course.

And I have seen golden eagles and swallows so ensnared,
the wind itself ensnared in these deftly woven nets
we obey as resignation, habit, and canon.
Fear is their champion,
these shadows of the recent past
who have come calling with their nets and brambles.
And they have taken the eagles from the heights,
placing them in cages fitted together
in perfect rows of conformity.

My two eyes have seen these pretenders,
caging the souls of eagles in their traps,
the horizon, blazing with its fire,
starved and waiting to encircle their wings again.

I was naked and young, wet and naïve,
in the dew of first light where
I never found knowledge, foresight, or language,
growing up from the soil beneath my naked feet.
The sunlight astonished me,
bouncing back and forth between all the shiny things.
This is how they kept my eyes distracted,
and how the heart was mesmerized with a lie,
the lie of one wearing the disguise of the only,
having us pretend that the myriad constellations
are but a figment of our imagination.

When I woke up from the twilight,
I saw with my own eyes,
the whole expanse of the blue-black sky,
heralding the rising and dance of stars,
spread out as fiery fingers
to the four directions of the universe.
I saw for myself the colors of the ancient Gods,
painted across the warp and the weft of the stellar loom.
And my heart remembered
the language it had lost
when it was young and wet and naïve.

I spread out my two arms wide
in the face of the jealous and angry law of the land.
And in the sacred stillness of my heart,
I heard the language of the primordial Gods,
beating and breathing.
Through the land, They beat and breathe.
Through the sky, They beat and breathe.
Through the air, They beat and breathe.
Through the waters of ocean and river,
They beat and breathe.
Through the birds soaring or alighting,
They beat and breathe.
Through my Mother's breast, They beat and breathe.
Through my Father's seed, They beat and breathe.
Through the language we have handed down
from the beginning,
They beat and They breathe.

"Such knowledge cannot be confounded by one,
nor disguised by the pall they have pulled over the eyes
of memory.
For the truth of memory is that it can be remembered,
and the truth of knowledge is that it can be recovered."
And this is what the dawn whispered
to my young and wet ears,
in the age of my naïve sight of all their shiny things.

One by one, and with my heart and fingers unleashed,
I severed the snares and released the traps
that the recent past had so deftly set.
The Sun came with me to witness, with its all-seeing eyes,
the return of eagles and swallows to their heights,
colors of fire and light at last,
dancing with one another through the unbounded veil,
in which the celebration of the stars could be seen.

Golden eagles, swallows and sparrows,
veil of luminescence beyond the play of shadow,
your wings, your heights returned to you,
your plummets having fallen
into the depths of the ancient sea.
You have all found my heart remembered,
in the place where it was lost,
irrecoverable, I once thought,
until I heard the voice of Spirit's memory
calling down through the keep of time.

Twilight, I play in your dusky veil.
Dawn, I come to your footfall renewed
from the spring of memory.
Air and Sun, I inhale your breath and make love
within your sacral embrace.
I have gone back to my beginning,
where the Gods in their memory
walk patiently through the ages.
I have gone back to our beginning,
where the memory of our Gods
walks patiently through our ages.

17: Flesh
Union With the Gods

The cup of our blood and our bones, in the beginning,
receives the brush of the maker's mark,
my Mother, having held me
compassionately to her breast of wisdom,
from whose lotus flower I drank,
when it sprang from the primordial mass.

Mother,
drawing my consciousness down from the celestial regions,
bestowed upon me her unwearying breath.
I carry this within me,
where the lungs that charge my blood,
draw Her in, draw Her out.

The cup of our loins from which lovers drink,
in the beginning bears the hallmark
of those primordial Gods,
who drank from the abyss of the Ancient Time,
who loved with the first flame,
from whose illumination creation was inspired.

My Father,
having steadied my bones against his stalwart chest,
bringing my skin the comfort of the terrestrial world,
he rooted my feet deep within the ancient soil
of that first mound of Earth,
to break with its crest the virgin sky hallowed,
receiving the soul of the Sky.
He stretched out his hands,
and gave to me the First Beginning in His seed.

Mother of the Sky,
I have received my inheritance
from the channels of your breast;
wherefrom the stars suspended,
in their bright courses draw forth
the divine light that guides us.
Wherefrom the ancient Earth seeks comfort
when its peaks lift up their sheer and stony faces;
wherefrom my hidden eye receives
the consolation of knowledge
the Ancestors read.

In my star-clad Mother, I find the language of all the ages
spelled out in perfect meter, Her sound that of instruments,
whose music becomes the fire of the Sun,
leaping across the horizons from dawn until dusk.
Sound that awakens the sleeping ears of the heart,
to hear what was woven
in the black abyss of the First Beginning.

Father of the Ancient Earth,
I have received my inheritance from
the potent meadows of your loins;
where sparrows alight,
to bring the knowledge they have gathered from the sky;
where hope is planted that grows in darkness,
shooting forth from its grave, the hallows of the World Tree;
where the Gods of the ancient time have taken counsel
to inscribe the names of every soul
upon the silver leaves of that enduring tree;
where the passions of the senses are born,
and in the end take their rest.

What rest have I in the bare and empty Earth,
when the stars of heaven seek to guide me
into their bodies of vital sight, and the earth itself,
being prone yet with eyes turned upward,
seeks its destiny from the dance of lights
spinning ages away?

I will become one of those lights,
when my time on the mountains is spent,
and the Earth has nothing more from memory to say.
I shall spin and I shall dance in the Sky,
taking about my shoulders a sapphire mantle spangled
with gilt lights to challenge Moon's vanity.

What need have I for sleep
in the caverns of jealous mountains,
when the Sky has come calling my name,
being the language that resurrects the desolate
crags and canyons of the deserts,
bringing back the ageless trees
from whose branches youth draws its evergreen promise?

I shout, not whisper, to the Sky,
when the light of stars opens up my eyes after twilight.
I weave the warp and the weft of language, not silence,
when the Earth gives up its Mysteries to my veins,
while the ears of my heart draw near to listen.

My face is the countenance of the Sun God,
indestructible gold, I cannot tarnish, nor be taken down
into that bottomless abyss from which the ancient Earth
was drawn.

My two eyes are the Sun and the Moon,
leading the day and guiding the night before me.
The seasons I take up with my reins firm in hand,
while the tides follow fast on my heels,
together with the hearts of all men.
My right eye is gold and my left eye silver,
ruddy carnelian and alabaster of milky luminescence,
wherefrom time and the tides draw forth their terrible power.

My two ears are the doors of Heaven,
up to which the ladder of the Sky rises from the heart.
What rises is the ancient cadence
of memory woven by the Ancients,
those stars and their kin,
whose faces in the vault dazzle the eyes of men.

These are the lights that fashion the rungs of the ladder
upon which souls rise.
So rise, you shadows and shades who have come after me!
Rise up from your depths in the keep of the Earth,
where light cannot reach you and life ceases to inhabit you.
Make your footfalls here in the embrace of my arms,
where you shall sprout the wings of sparrows,
flying golden and unencumbered
upon the virgin breath of spring.

Is this not what the stars portended by their courses,
when the Earth was not yet ancient,
and the heavens danced their first dance
in the company of solitude.

Moon, you found us there,
springing up from the hallows of the Earth
with our sparrow's wings,
the Sun behind us in his mountainous horizon.

We beheld that moon and those stars with our fresh eyes,
painted only by the flaxen light
of Heaven's crown and Her jewels
these jewels our own inheritance
when we learn the language to decipher them.

This is what my Mother gave me from Her breast,
what our Mother gave us when She cracked open the heavens
for the sustenance of our hungry lips.

This is what our Father passed down to us in His seed,
what our Father gifted our loins,
when He gave the far-reaching roots of the Earth
to our striving feet.

The cup of our blood and our bones in the beginning
receives the brush of the maker's mark,
our Mother, having held us as the stars,
to Her celestial breast,
giving us the language of the sky,
to take with us on our travels,
our Father, having whispered the knowledge of memory
through His earthly seed,
and this to carry with us on our travels through the air.

For we are sparrows with golden wings,
carrying Heaven in our breast
when we alight upon the Earth.
And it is only after we land that we come to forget
the language of Heaven that guided us from whence we came.

18: Coming Forth By Day

I have left my body behind,
in the Earth that hungers for flesh and bone,
flesh of my mother's keeping, transfigured into an effigy,
bone of my father's shaping, silent as a stone by the wayside.
Am I now a cold lamp guttering,
as eventide clothes the mountains?
Am I spirited from my skin and blood,
to become a dusky shadow of those mountains
my eyes have always seen from a distance?

There is no distance now,
between I and the mountains, brooding;
between I and the wayside, littered with stones;
between I and the black soil, cold without life's footfall;
between I and the cavernous hallows;
where the Sun-God is swallowed.
Now I am swallowed beyond the joys of the earthly banks,
where life does not tarry.

I come to the gap in the silent Earth,
where the fragile body of the Sun-God
is swallowed by his starry mother,
the ebony plaits of her hair swinging low,
as the net of the naked sky.
Her fecund breasts hang down to meet my parched lips,
these wanderers in the darkness with my tongue taking suck,
fed by the luminescence of constellations in her net.
"Drink! Drink!" These dancing fires say to me.
"Fill your mouth with memory,
that you may know where you have been!"

But my body has long since departed.
Or is it what was within my body that has departed,
to become a spectral light wandering?
It is the Sun-God who wanders with me
into the Mother's celestial hallow,
his aged and shaggy body like that of an old ram.
"Ba! Ba!," sing the stars in their net as he passes
glinting as silver, his creaking bones through his skin,
flashing as copper and gold,
through the dust of the ages, his flesh
brittle yet vivid to my downturned eyes,
his locks of lapis lazuli.

"You have at last found your father," the Sun-God said to me,
"who is received in the West when twilight comes
to kiss the Two Banks with her starry lips.
And you have found your Mother.
You enter the mouth of your Mother who receives you;
who swallows you whole as she swallows
the bodies of memory, past and present;
who swallows all that is spoken
in the past and what is yet to come;
whose hunger encircles the Earth and knows no limits;
whose body is time and whose stars
are the future courses of the Earth;
whose constellations unveil the seeds of distant ages;
whose ages are the roots of a great tree,
where the Sun goes to die."

But he is reborn from the crown of its branches,
which pierce the flank of the Sky and draw forth Her lights.
She is the Sky of the First Beginning,
this Mother into whom I descend.
She who gulps down the stars and the swollen Moon,
all dancing for her in their orbits around the vault.
She is the Mother who gave me my true and secret name
the name that contains every memory since time began.

The Sun-God was swallowed before my very eyes
naked and bereft of all light,
naked of flesh and sensual blood.
I found the crocodile in his place, whose jaws spanning miles
held the quivering light of the Moon.
"I swallow the Moon-God when he has grown bloated,"
crocodile said to me,
"when he has grown fat with memory,
and competes with the stars for their light.
I devour innocence as the fresh flowers on the bank,
the wind which comes from the promise of harvest;
the black earth from which green shoots spring
the pregnant soil of the Two Banks,
which know the memory of life;
the sycamore whose leaves foretell the future,
and whose roots cling to the past;
youth and its seasons of dalliance and pleasure experience,
which itself is fragile as the shell of an egg.
All of these I devour at will, like I devour the Moon-God,
and grow swollen upon his luster."

To greedy old crocodile I said,
"I shall plant myself in the black mud of my Father's body,
and during the twilight hours I shall transform into a lotus,
a lotus of the primordial blue of the Ancient Waters,
where are found all the things that endure the ages.
For you are the hunger of age and time,
which are never sated and can never be veiled.
There are nightfall and eclipse which hunger for the Sun;
drought and famine which hunger for the Earth
locust and rat which hunger for the corn;
fire and flood which hunger for the verdant fields;
barrenness and impotence which hunger for the generations;
loneliness and despair which hunger for the heart;
and you are death and putrefaction,
which ever hunger for the substance of life and form.

"But I have been given memory from the milk of my Mother,
and I have been given knowledge from the seed of my Father,
these things which are passed down and inherited
within the keep of the Mysteries.
The Sky keeps them according to the courses of the stars,
who spell out in their journeys
the language in which memory speaks.
And this language is unknown to death and dissolution,
which cannot unveil the uncreated nor devour the formless.
I become that sky-blue lotus, clad in the Ancient Waters,
before time, age, and form came into being,
thus, the Sun-God is conceived in my belly,
and disperses his light to scatter the crocodiles of the abyss."

Crocodile is eaten,
by the first golden beams of the eastern sky,
piercing the iron scales of his body like gilded barbs.
What death and extinction fear most is memory,
the intangible language of the ages,
which twitters in the ears of time,
as do swallows in the eaves by sundown.
Come little swallow, hearty and vociferous,
and give your memory to become
the language of my new lips
to pronounce the secret name of the Sun-God,
hidden within the keep of the stars!

What Swallow whispers, in my wet ears,
is the conversation of the abyss,
which was first heard by the Gods,
that in darkness we find our beginning,
secreted from the life of forms,
forms that dissipate and know time, and age, and death,
as all that becomes form shall know.
But the created shall migrate into the uncreated,
which is light before is passes over into the seen world;
which is seed before it bursts
into the green shoots of the field;
which is sound before it is received by the ears;
which is the wind before it stirs the waters;
which is the sky after dusk and before the Sun rises;
which is gold, untarnished and not birthed
by the hand of man;
which is language before it is written or spoken;
which is thus memory,
transferred from form to form to form,
outside time, and age, and death.

Swallow has become a falcon of gold
absorbed by the sky,
whose wings now taste the courses stars have traveled.
To become as He I must look to the patterns
that dance through my fingers,
illumination that plays upon the Earth at our feet,
and above our heads, spells out that secret name
of the uncreated Sun-God.

With darkness as my womb and light as my guide,
I pass down through my many ages
where the uncreated hide.
Reaching far back before the birth of my form,
to recover the pattern of language
from which memory is born.

19: *Return to the Waters of Life*

And I found myself confronting the great abyss,
those raging waters that have existed
before the presence of living beings,
churning between the lofty banks of the sky,
yet without form or bottom.
I could no longer see the Earth and its mountains,
hard spires of stone rising to pierce
the delicate flank of the venerated Sky,
her face and naked form now lost to me
as I entered the deep.

Am I a child again, lonely and crestfallen beneath the void,
my bare toes finding fear in the taste of water,
where wait all the things I have left behind me?
Mother Sky, once spread out,
like a sapphire loom above my brow,
your dazzling fabric with its constellations for thread,
has been unraveled before my eyes,
no longer seeing your path of light.
Father Earth, the seed of mountains and the caverns
lurking beneath the tempestuous waves,
I have lost my foothold in your ancient skin,
my comfort in your keep.

Having seen the Sun-God swallowed by his mother,
I searched for his trail of fire upon the waters,
seeking the past, security in what has been;
seeking the present, security in what one knows;
seeking the future, security in what one expects will be.

But there is no lamp and no flame,
no gilt promise spilling over these waters.
These waters we face alone, when our moment comes,
without Mother or Father to guide us.
We are naked in the preeminent abyss,
where time itself is devoured.

My sparrow found me from his secret nest,
hidden in the folds of the clouds.
These I could not see,
and yet his little wings brought him to me.
"What do you carry with you,"
he chirped in the ears of my heart?
My heart leaped into my mouth,
and overcame the prudence of my lips.
"I carry with me fear, judgment, and guile."
Sparrow heard these three raptors call out their names
from the echoing jar of my heart.
I heard my transgressions afresh,
all waiting to peck and tear at my flesh.
"You are a jade," I heard the Sky call,
though I could not see the Sky's watery countenance.
"You are a broken vessel," I heard the Earth murmur,
though I could not see the Earth beneath the angry tide.
"You have swallowed your heart,"
I heard the mountains grumble,
though I could not see their indomitable towers
rising to meet the sky.
"You have let your heart be carried away by other hands,"
Sparrow said to me,
as his gentle wings enfolded my heart's vessels.

But my impetuous heart carried me in its boat,
across waters that swam with the serpents of the deep.
Their iron scales broke the surface of the abyss
to send the thunder of their names tearing through the wind.
Void, negligence, and destruction
turned through the waters of despair,
who could not allow a single piece of land
to rise peacefully in their midst.
How I had tasted them throughout my many travels
drinking their vigor.
I felt myself immune to their inebriation,
and their beds I visited with relish in my loins.

"The Sun-God came here at the First Occasion,"
Sparrow said to me,
"Bursting through the wet fist of that burgeoning lotus,
his eager member formed a body of golden light,
its radiant beams dividing the waters
strangled by serpent's coils.
Sky was heralded, who parted the dusky veil of her lips
to proclaim the first dawn,
growing ruddy on the new horizon.
Her pangs of birth shuddered the wind into motion.
The infant Earth responded
by lifting up into manhood to meet her,
a fresh and new earth hailing a sky
in motion with the dancing of stars."

I want to be one of those unsullied and whirling stars,
to make love to a virgin sky;
to find that lotus of the First Occasion
as a bud yet unbroken;
to float on water unencumbered
by the anchor of the past;
to cut the ties of jaded experience
weighing down my naked toes;
to open my eyes with the Sun;
to find the years of my life stretching ahead,
not to have discarded a single moment
chasing regret, indecision, or waste.
These are the droplets of sorrow that have filled
the jug of my heart to brimming.
It has no room for hope or conviction or abundance.

Heron, with eyes blazing, sought me out upon the abyss.
Known for wise contemplation
and dispelling the shroud of darkness,
His feathers still bore the wet tidings of the flood,
the First Occasion of beginnings,
when the Earth met the Sky in frantic abandon.
"I remove you to the Mound,
where the history of the world began,
its innocence pushing up from the black soil of Flood's keep.
This is the Flood who was summoned
by the movements of Sun-God's hand,
His body enthused by the pang of golden loins.

Here lies the secret of the First Beginning,
where sprouted the Gods
from the language of that sky-blue lotus.
Memory being its name, when it first touched the unclad sky
with its petals of sound and word.
Know the Mound and you will know the Waters of Life,
which defeat the footfall of death."

After an age I reached the place of the Mound,
cutting up through the twisting abyss,
with flank and lofty crown of gold,
its beauty dressed my eyes.
Dark water did not know the Mound,
nor how to pronounce its name.
Thus the Mound could push its way
through the torrent and remain.
For it is sound that frightens the chaotic abyss,
which seeks only to strangle,
it finds its hold on any kernel of light,
to choke out its fragile life.
It is from voice and word that language forms
to divide its jealous fingers creation,
flowering from the bud that grows
within the gap the waters leave.

Now seen by the Mound and the Gods that stand upon it,
I climb to the place where Heron has his gilded nest,
where the reflection of Mother Sky shines across the waters;
where beams of turquoise light strike down
through the jagged rocks below;
where Water with his wet lips reaches up
to kiss the florid cheek of Sky;
where my disassembled form finds consolation
in the body of the Sun.

"You have carried in your hands the filth a heart swallows,"
say the Twin Gods to me,
"and I know that filth has names
like jaded, ignorance, and forgetfulness."
The first of Twin Gods,
whose head was a golden falcon declared,
"I take from you the weighty drops
of scorn that have choked your heart.
I make room for the water of nobility,
which floats to the top above rancor!"
From a vessel of fine gold
he poured over my sky-clad shoulder
the water he had called forth from the Flood.
The second of Twin Gods, whose head
was a turquoise wading bird declared,
"I take from you the stupefying drops
of forgetfulness that have nullified your heart.
I make room for the water of intelligence,
which rises to the top above ignorance!"
From a vessel of burnished silver
he poured over my moon-clad shoulder
the water he had called forth from the flood.

I brought with me the cup of sorrow,
I fill it with joy.
I brought with me the cup of tears,
I fill it with laughter.
I brought with me the cup of spite,
I fill it with tenderness.
I brought with me the cup of hatred,
I fill it with love.
I brought with me the cup of jealousy,
I fill it with compassion.
I brought with me the cup of possession,
I fill it with generosity.
I brought with me the cup of exclusion,
I fill it with openness.
I brought with me the cup of persecution,
I fill it with acceptance.
I brought with me the cup of ignorance,
I fill it with knowledge.
I brought with me the cup of inexperience,
I fill it with wisdom.
I brought with me the cup of silence,
I fill it with language.
I brought with me the cup of indifference,
I fill it with memory.

Having been filthy for ages with the ignorance of the veil,
my unclad eyes saw my glistening new skin with wonder,
so like the skin I inherited from my Mother
when she gave me to the world;
so like the form I received from my Father,
when his hands urged me forward.

How purity finds us even after we fall by the wayside,
the dirt of the heart refusing to be shed,
and how we go to the grave long before our body dies.
It is forgetfulness that weaves
the warp and the weft of suffering.
We peer at the world
through the opaque shroud of our making,
placing at the doorsteps of others the loom our life gave us.
But we are the weavers,
carrying the hands our Gods made us,
who spoke for us the language of a soul,
and the immortality of memory
traveling down through the ages.

It is I who return my body to the Flood from which it came,
shrinking back the small mind from which ignorance is made.
It is I who place the sightless veil
over eyes in my own keeping,
and I who wash away the veil
from eyes of memory sleeping.

20: Entering the Hidden Chamber

I come now into your presence in darkness,
returning to the wet womb of my Mother,
to swim in the flood of the First Beginning,
where rose the Primordial Gods upon the sacral mound.
The flood has taken me by the hand
and from the veil of death,
which blankets the stars and seeks life's consolation.
But I have swallowed down those wandering constellations
to become an imperishable star.
Darkness, I wander no longer in your void.

The Gods have kept their mount in secret,
within the hallow of all hallows embracing the ancient Earth.
Below, black earth, the traveling companion of my bare feet,
father of all my fathers who alone was with the Sun-God
when He uplifted his brightening eyes from the waters.
I have seen those waters now with my own two eyes,
churning and crashing with terror
before the emerging mountain.
These are the secrets of the First Beginning in my keep,
memory being in my confidence,
language being my beloved.

Above, sky of lapis lazuli,
thighs of gold of my Goddess suspended.
Her belly, the dancing ground of myriad constellations.
Her navel, the shrine where the Sun-God dazzles
in turquoise mantle.
Her black cleft,
the Mooring Post of the Sun's twilight barque.
Her flooded gap, the eastern portal,
where ascends the nascent sovereign.
Her breasts, the Twin Sycamores,
the pylons where the Sun-God is suckled.
Her dusky throat, the boughs of the tamarisk
in which the wind resides.
Her hair, cast out into the void as a net of gilt stars.
And these the places where the Earth longs to stride,
where all those born of creation's mound struggle to ascend.

Below my feet is that black Earth,
whose arms stretch out to meet Her.
She being the starry Mother,
from whose flooded thighs we wander.
Born of soil is this corpse
we borrow from the hands of our Father.
But we are the sparrows who alight for a precious time,
until the voice of the constellations
calls back our stellar body.
We know the ancient language of sparrows,
passed down from time's beginning,
which gave the Gods from their own tongues
before our star descended.

Our portion is to recall the language of that First Occasion,
hurled by the Sun-God
into those turbulent waters of the void,
His speech becoming the shimmering dance
of millions of stars.
These stars belong not only to the primordial Gods,
not only to the Sun-God upon His ocean lotus;
not only to the spray of water making love to the void;
not only to the wind whose kisses find the water wanting;
not only to the blue-black sky hurled far above the soil;
not only to the turquoise beams
striking the breast of the Earth;
not only to the Moon
whose crescent lips call out the seasons;
not only to the desert mountains of piercing spires;
not only to the river at flood time following in their wake;
not only to the rosy-gold dawn making ruddy the horizon;
and not only to the Mistress of Heaven
in whose keeping they shine.
These stars are our inheritance before Earth's soil knows us,
our two feet hailing from above before they know below.

Our first language is a stellar memory
woven from the net of stars.
Our heart, the Mooring Post
where the Ark of the Sun is fastened.
Our first words are that bull's thigh
through which we ascend.
We follow in the luminous entourage,
vitalizing the dark waters of the sky.
Our first body is that holy star becoming horizon's guide,
the East which hails us at the breaking of dawn,
calling the New Year Home.

Our life upon the Earth
is the mirror of the Unwearying Stars.
Day and night behold our comings and goings
in the upper and lower regions.
Our climax of yearning loins is the Milky Way,
ornament of Heaven's veil.
This is our veil of our astral wanderings,
to which we may return.
These are our stars, our bodies,
our Mother's net of our birthing,
and these are our first words, our first language,
our many before the coming of one.

My portion is now to remember the reading of the stars,
in whose net of language the memory of humankind is kept,
where we have journeyed in their footsteps,
gathering the knowledge of the Gods;
where we have traveled the course of the Sun-God,
making passage through the waters of the hours below;
where we have become swallows nesting
on the Sun's golden barge, the keepers of His secret language,
maintained by heaven's hallows;
where we have received the cleansing of the Milky Way,
its milk my Mother's breast, its flood my father's seed.

Having made my passage through the body of the vault,
I now come to the leaves of earthly doors
where the voice of Heaven follows.
The scent of myrrh knows my skin and my sweat is its savor,
this fragrance of verdant land and desert;
this embrace of the sycamore and tamarisk;
this love making of Earth and Sky;
this breath of the morning dew and night wind;
this diadem of the triumphant Sun and swollen Moon;
this eye of the upper world in its wholeness;
this eye of the lower world in its divisions;
these names of the primordial Gods
hidden within the keep of the Mound.
I am all of these powers of Theirs,
inherited by the stars of my body,
which shine in the night sky unhindered by the shadows.
See me shine you Gods of the indwelling magic,
and receive this body of light within Your bodies of light!

I come now to the leaves of heavenly doors,
entering through the Earth of my ancient Father,
His flesh the black soil between my naked toes.
I bear upon my arms the fresh dew of the ruddy dawn,
making me as a babe suckling at his mother's breast.
The flood of her thighs has brought me to the hidden mound,
where the language of swallows fills my empty ears.
These wet ears of mine,
now swimming in the primordial chorus.

We came first from the ocean of many,
where all stars have their home.
From millions in a net of lights
these swallows alight alone.
Return to the mound of beginnings
is the destiny of the one,
where one becomes the many again,
where the journey is undone.

21: *Awakening the Hidden Chamber*

I bring you sound as the language of becoming,
sound, being the warp and the weft of our beginning,
sprouting from the abyss of the unknown;
sound, the footfall of those tempestuous waters,
abounding with the serpents of the deep;
sound, from the milk of your starry Mother,
Her body held up for you when you were the infant Sun;
sound, the chorus of your great eye when it opened,
to illumine the shadows of the uncreated world;
sound, the light of your eye in its many divisions,
bringing together the two halves of the pristine sky;
sound, the rapturous union of Earth and Sky,
the Ancient Mound and star-strewn vault of our First Time;
sound, the loins of my Father,
awake and held firm in his hand;
sound, the thighs of my Mother,
yawning and glistening with golden dew;
sound, Father's wet shudder
as the Imperishable Stars burst forth;
sound, Mother's call,
when the two door leaves of heaven are thrown open;
sound, the swallows at the prow of the Night Ark,
calling out the serpent from his coils;
sound, the swallows at the prow of the Day Ark,
conversing with the Sun-God
as the horizons unfurl before him;
sound, the light-gorged vessel of my heart in your presence,
having received the turquoise Sun
upon the skin of my two arms;

sound, reaching out to embrace you,
like that flared hood of the Cobra-Goddess;
sound, the waves of water and luminescence
of your triumphant eye.

I bring my two hands as the eastern and western horizons,
the two horizons, shining as burnished gold
when your countenance passes,
your double eye capturing the lapis lazuli of the sky;
the two horizons, wet with the flood of the first beginning,
whose lakes of gold and silver
carry aloft your disk and crescent faces;
the two horizons, the Twin Sycamores
of lofty and piercing boughs,
standing to face the ruddy dawn,
when its sun-calf strides between them;
the two horizons, the eastern eye
which captures the Earth at daybreak,
and the western eye which ensnares the dusky sky in its net;
the two horizons, the tamarisk from which the sky pours,
and the sycamore in which the constellations seek refuge;
the two horizons, the sky-blue lotus
of the Sun's ancient birth,
the blue-black mound where his golden hawk alighted;
the two horizons, these two pylons
between which my arms extend,
bringing with them the light and darkness
of the first beginning.

Hear O Gods the voice of my heart,
resounding in the shadows
as the wholesome eye of the dawn!
What I have chased is the injury upon me,
clouding my heart like the blearing of your celestial eye,
closing the door leaves of the sky to my gaze.
But I have thrown open the gates of the sky before you,
the eastern and western veils
rent from the lights of your eyes.
In the East your door leaves are thrown
wide open with the Sun.
Your door leaves in the West are thrown
wide open at your approach.
The yawning legs of the sky present
their verdant mound to you,
its eventide fissure making wet the path
your holy feet tread.
I inhale the cloud of your lotus fragrance
diffused from your loins,
this the scent of that very first dawn
breaking the leaves of the sky.

Hear O Gods the beating of my heart,
the light that unfurls your heart's ears!
I come on the tide of those ancient waters
where the face of the Sun shone forth,
His arousal stirring the body of the flood,
His hand summoning the wind with its commands.
I come as His hand and His command,
my sacral tread bringing with it
that light of the first beginning.
Let the lights of my two eyes shine for you in the darkness,
traveling the course of the Unwearying Stars before you.

Let the command of my two lips
place the Imperishable Stars in your keep,
their illumination the mooring post,
where the light of the world gleams.

Hear O Gods the language of the sky,
pregnant with memory through the glance of eternal stars!
She is the Mother who bore the heavens and uplifted the Sun,
Her breast the sanctuary of untold constellations.
Stretching out Her two arms,
She cradled the dewy mantle of the Sun,
breathing into his mouth the fragrance of your beginning.
Through half moon lips was the vault,
ordered according to her wish,
the Sun becoming the sovereign
of the naked and virgin horizon.
Come Sun and come horizon,
you thigh of bull and perch of falcon,
where the ruddy mantle of the dawn pours out at your feet!
Your language is the color of the midnight sky,
whose sound is the dance of the Unwearying Stars
rising and falling, yet rising again.

I too rise after I have fallen.
See my body rising as a heron to crown the brow of heaven.
Behold my wings of gold riding the wind as a falcon.
Hear my words as a swallow breaking the silence of the Sky.
For when your Earth has fallen beneath my bare feet,
when the stillness of the waters has covered the Two Banks,
I will rise as a star in the eastern portion of Heaven,
and my portion shall be the whole of the Sun's course
through the belly of his starry Mother.

Take the lamp of my full face and its light,
having filled the horizons and dazzled the green Earth,
its beauty bears the language of that first daybreak,
coming fast over the rolling hills
where the Sun dances before us.
Let us dance when the Sun-God dances over his soil,
rich in His life and potent in His savor,
with sycamore and tamarisk swaying in our wake!
See how His light plies
the southern waters from their dusky slumber,
awakened by the shout of His celestial eye,
they flood the Earth's rolling hills with their ancient
memory.

Now you rise and awake like that ancient flood,
bringing upon your youthful skin
the blue essence of first light's lotus.
And who is born from the dew of its unfolding petals,
who becomes the child of the flood,
from which the Sky draws its fire?
I am held at the breast of that sun-clad flower,
to shine my face upon the lonely waters of the world.
It is the Sky who opens its two eyes before me,
and the Earth who extends his body to receive me.

I bring you sound as the language of becoming,
to open up your ears.
I bring you light as the memory of beginning,
to reckon millions of years.
I bring you my heart's constant beating,
to fill the empty spaces.
I bring my heart's most ancient flood
to awaken your dark spaces.

22: Walking With Date Palms

Remove the veil from my eyes, O Sky,
so that I, like you in your finest hour,
may peer out openly at the ascending stars,
whose charted courses still appear
mysterious to my virgin eyes,
stripped now of their illusions and in wonder like a child.
I need no veil to disguise my intentions,
no cloud or mantle to hide away my heart from sunset.
He comes to greet me with fiery gold upon his shoulders,
the west wind at his back.
The desert in its jealous rages
is quelled by his upright footsteps.

He greets me with the song of sparrows
weaving through his clouds,
those ruddy clouds dancing above
the sovereign cliffs and mountains,
bestowing their sand to the winds as a chafing gift.
But still I need no veil to hide my naked shoulders.
I would rather wear the cape of the indomitable Sky,
whose only industry is to make love to the Sun,
to cradle the clouds that come to rise
upon the celestial waters;
to give the eastern horizon
a mirror to sit upon its golden throne;
to give starry Mother a child to swallow
when he descends the western horizon;
to give the constellations a veil of lapis lazuli
for their glittering limbs.
It is they, not I, who don the twilight veil
to become the house of Mysteries.

I have walked alone, these many and opaque ages,
many lifetimes with the pall of ignorance as my inheritance,
with eyes that are open yet carry no sight.
How much cooler to embrace the desert's mirage
than brave the sands for what they are.
Should I take up that veil again to soften the Sun's glare,
his eager stare blazing over my tender skin
like the heat of a lover?
I would rather kiss his fingers where they fall,
offer him the cool luxury of my bed,
these before I would shield his existence
from my exposed purpose.

Having run away from the Sun when I was only a child,
I turn now and face his scathing embrace.
And what I find in the florid sky is a mirror reflecting
the tread of my careless feet through this world.
Burning through the skins of others,
I have become the desert sun.
All along it was never I who needed the veil's protection,
but the eyes of others whose hearts were burned by my stare.

Now I am walking with date palms,
whose fruit like gemstones falls in my waiting lap.
Justice is loyal to herself.
She follows the hands that work for the tree,
wherever they have traveled.
Tears are the bounty she brings,
for the eyes that have caused them fear
is the edge of her sword drawn to the shield.

Held against her thirst is the glance of her ample bosom,
held out for the mouth that opposed her.
But she requites with favor the heart
that knows her noble labors.
She bestows in kind what the heart has to give her.

Shall I hold out two doves in my waiting hands,
offering to you the peace
that wind brought me from the tender North?
Have you heard their cooing voices,
so like the persuasions of my heart when it joins you?
You who have become a journeyer with me,
whose eyes have looked east to face the blazing sun;
You whose feet have tread the thorny and fallen boughs;
You whose lips have ached to kiss my half moon lips;
You whose hands have held the wandering stars to guide me;
You whose arms have never faltered
to keep my sky suspended;
You whose names have moved my lips
when my knees drew the earth;
You whose words twittered in my ears
with the language of sparrows;
You whose wings found wind and sky
beckoning above my brow;
You in whose keeping the hallowed Mysteries
have remained inviolate.
You have moved your feet
on the blare of the desert wind beside me,
and I lift up my two hands to offer you
the refuge of my heart.

I lift up my open palm of water to the thirsty sky,
and through its miracle I feed the world.
There is no desert left in me,
for you to brave with starving feet.
There are no stones for you to cross in your path.
There are no mountains to tear the veil of your peaceful sky.
There is no flame hidden from your cold hands,
when the Sun is devoured.
There is no torrent to blot out
the starry courses that go before you.
There is no endless journey in the sky,
for the swallow's wings of your soul.
There are no labors in the Sun,
without the Moon to reward them.
There is no Heaven without
the illumination of stars to light it.
These all may be found for you
in the open palm of my hand,
which carries the miracle of water
to quench the thirsty sky.

Shelter me as does the Earth to mountains,
not in my time of weakness,
but when my heart climbs high with fortitude.
I am a date palm in the wind of your adept fingers.
My fruit falls into your waiting hands,
as do stars through the dusky veil.

The veil cannot hold them, those stars of brilliant ages,
whose lamps form a trail of gold across a lapis dome.
And no veil can contain the far-striding feet of my heart,
light upon the pathways of the Earth when nearing you.
If that canopy above us remains parched by the desert gale,
then we will lift up our open palms of water
to the thirsty sky.
And through our miracle, we will feed the world.

Now we are walking with date palms,
stripped of our illusions and in wonder like a child.
This is our finest hour,
beholding the ascending stars
with fresh and virgin eyes,
as they ascend with millions of ages.
They come down through the paths of the desert sky,
as they have always done.

And we come back through the paths of the desert earth,
as we have always done.
We need no veil to disguise our intentions,
our stars glistening in their ancient courses.
We need no mantle to clothe our eyes,
walking with date palms through the desert crossroads.
We need only open our palms of water to the thirsty sky,
and through our miracle, we will feed the world.

23: Many Where We Are Made

Between the four pillars of the sky,
I have found the home that loves me.
Its torches burn as lamps held high,
above the flickering shadows of mountains.
His feet have pulled me, this Earth upon whom I tread.
Her lips have kissed my languid skin,
this Sky beneath whom I slumber,
enveloping my mortal nature with hers of sacred endurance.

Within the winds of the four directions,
I have heard the voice of memory calling.
It weaves into my heart the ancient language of past ages.
Lips lit by moonlight fill my ears with wind's beginning,
the wind that opens the palm of my hand
to receive its rousing fruit.
I have shaken its dusky trees
by the light of the summer moon,
when lovers with yawning thighs held me fast in their gale.
Still I gathered your fruit in my empty fingers,
while wise men chided my mortal hunger.

"There are no winds and no lips," these wise men declare.
"It is a sin to count the immeasurable stars,
and blasphemy to love them!"
And how many of these wise men
will endure the twilight ages,
when the stars in their brilliant courses shine on?
Show me but a single star in the midnight sky,
and I will show you but a single sky to receive its holy light.

I beheld the eastern sky
suffused with a mirror's burnished glare,
its gold foretold the coming of the Sun
into the heaven of morning.
I have shielded my eyes from the molten glance
of electrum over the vault,
its two metals heralding the afternoon sky
to the timid earth below.
I have seen the azure veil
streaked with eventide's ruddy fire,
the western horizon going down
to its rest in a blaze of heavenly ardor.
How many skies from how many directions
have guided my wandering eyes?
How many lights from how many lamps
have shown my heart its way?
Still those wise men tell me there is but a single sky,
there is but a single flame burning with only a single life.

The Moon holds me in its alabaster fingers,
as its footfall holds the tides.
By night I am naked to many lovers,
shining upon its cloak.
Tides and lovers are pulled by its mirror,
to usher Heaven in.
Both are received by my longing eyes,
which travel heaven and skin.
What difference are tides or moon to my eyes,
when both bring lovers calling?
Wise men speak of but a single light
when my eyes have seen them falling.

Moon, I cannot hold you too tightly in my grasp,
when you are summoned by the horizons
to be their constant lover.
You travel far from my fawning eyes and roaming hands,
yet return with your full face reflected
in the stillness of my garden pool.
But your countenance in the sky
is like your reflection on water,
vanishing when the tips of my eager fingers
touch your ivory cheek.
Are you the very same Moon when you return to the veil,
wearing your face as a crescent?
Like the tides your light shrinks and swells,
while the horizons drink your savor.
Wise men say that you are one and alone,
with full or crescent reflection.
Their hands have never tasted the myriad lips
kissing Heaven's waters.

Shall I disappear with you beyond that veil of water,
only to return with full face lighted by your sacral fire?
I have summoned you each night
with words of that ancient tongue,
accompanied by the chime of memory
and the song of remembrance.
That veil you wear in which are secreted
the Mysteries of my ages,
I part with deft hands
guided by memories of my many forms.

These once carried names like abandonment and destitution.
I accepted the fate imposed by their one,
when many waited beyond.
I saw my two hands empty,
when my heart overflowed before me.
Still I drank their wisdom,
without respite for my parched lips.
Your language piqued my hands
to lift the memories through the veil,
and I heard names like reclamation and abundance
thundering as drums.
Why would I see a single sky,
when East and West embrace me?
How could I follow a single light,
when millions shine to guide me?

My naked feet dance in the face
of that garden pool by lamplight,
bringing with them the joy of stars
whirling in their courses.
I ask the wise men if they have tasted
the potent fruit of doum palms,
tumbling in a summer night's breeze
with the taste of lovers between them.
My open palms have taken the fruit
from trees that pierced the sky.
My eyes have gathered the curves of hearts
poured out on the empty sands.
My naked feet never whirled alone
with sequins on that mantle,
with stars like gemstones in my company
heralding your many names.

Come myrrh and anoint my limbs
with kisses of the Gods,
their lights to gleam as stars
from my loins below a silver navel.
I strip my neck of all its jewels
with Full Moon as my brother,
his hands of light sliding like gold
to reach my garden pool.
Am I not decorated by Heaven each night
when Moon becomes my lover?
I find respite in the ardor of stars
whose untiring fingers bless me.

Where have I danced before this age,
moved my feet with constellations?
I have come from a stifling pool,
whose waters doused my guiding fires.
But East and West still held their flames
before my seeking eyes,
their sights by day and night
found me wandering beneath the sky.
Sun, you witness arms stretched out
to fill the space between us.
Moon, you come and find me,
where I move in sacred time.
Your names I have taken with your fruit falling on the winds,
their voices calling out the many from the age of one.

The pillars of the sky hold up the vault
where my feet come to tread,
with mountains framing each horizon,
where their mirrors gleam.
I bring with unclad toes the language of my becoming,
my many ages pouring from their hands of fragrant memory.
My heart is now a tree of myrrh
where a desert once portended.
Its jealous one holding prisoner
the green of youth I sought.
Wise men told me their pasture
held the only green worth having.
My stars outshone them all by nightfall
when a million lights flowered.

Between the four pillars of the sky
is found the home where I am carried,
a tree of sight in which the light
of Sun and Moon are married.
Their torches burn beneath the horizon
where twined are light and shade,
to join the tree where grow the souls
from many where we are made.

24: Where the Sun Finds His Sanctuary

I depart from the doorways of this world
without consolation of the things I have known.
A stranger in my own flesh, do I own my flesh?
A stranger beneath the sky, am I beneath my sky?
A stranger to the breath in my lungs,
is there breath in my lungs?
A stranger to the beating of my heart,
is that the beating of my heart?
Or am I now a corpse in that place
they call the hallowed West,
where the Sun-God comes in his old age
to meet the mouth of His Mother?

Mother, I remember your body
from before the day I was born.
It was your lake I swam in,
nourished by the flood of my beginning.
What you passed to me was the wet breath of my mortality,
the language of clinging to my body
of the earth before I knew Earth.
But I knew my fingers, my toes,
my mouth, and my beating heart.
It was your heart I heard in my flooded ears
swimming in the drum
through nine moons beating.

Mother, I remember the taste of your milk in my mouth,
your breasts of the sky feeding my lips constellations.
How the unwearying stars traverse the roof of my mouth
as they traverse the sky from dawn until dusk.
It was your milk that gave me the stars of the midnight hour,
these passing down to me the memory of our first beginning,
when we traveled the canals of the waters above.

Mother, you are my waters and you are my flood.
Carry me in your breast, and between your golden thighs.
Mother, you are the secret cavern where I will be reborn.
Call me to your cleft of the Gods where I will become a god.
Mother, yours is the mouth in which the Sun is swallowed.
Take me in your lips of sunset,
where I will shine as nether sky's mirror.

Mistress of the Sky, Mansion of Heaven, the Lady of Gold,
whose starry belly reckons the years of gods and men,
I cannot be a stranger when I come to your dusky flank,
for my face glitters in the shadows
like the Sun-God's reflection,
I being the child of your sky, the seed of your holy cavern,
the very memory of your celestial form.

When I go in by night,
I shine as one of those imperishable stars,
your body my ladder and your hands my enchantments.
But when I come out I go forth by day
as the light of the eastern horizon,
your flood my beginning,
and your birth pangs my heart's revival.

O Mother, be the sky stretched above my brow of gold,
and let your two arms clear a passage for me
through the waters on high!
Shout for me, lift me up on the curve
of your glittering thighs of metal,
and pronounce my name as a sacred star
to dazzle on your horizon.

House of the Gods,
Residence of the hawk,
Sanctuary of the Sun,
in which the bodies of the living Gods are fashioned forever.
You cannot remain a secret
from my two eyes when they find you.
For my eyes are the mirrors of the sky,
birthed from your keep.
My right eye opened by day
as the sovereign of the turquoise East.
My left eye opened by night
as the sovereign of the lapis West.
It is my eyes that know gold and master lapis lazuli,
and my body that sprouts turquoise
as the beams of the afternoon sun.

Gods of the western horizon,
hear my footsteps and remember my form.
Born from the same Mother who gave you birth,
my body spreading the savor of the nether sky before me,
the sheen of my skin inherited from the flesh of the Sun-God,
the iridescence of my flank being that of the sacred beetle,
my loins possessing the flood
that came forth from the beginning,
carrying between my thighs the Mound

where the Great Ba-Soul rose,
my brow being the vertex of the Lord to the Limits,
the crown of my head
being the horizon of the Cobra-Goddess,
and all of these forms of mine
being the very members of the Gods.

I enter the doorways of the West in the company of the stars,
going before me to proclaim my names to the eternal sky.
And I too am eternal,
in the body of the heavens where I am born.
This is my breath you hear, O Gods,
it expands the lungs of the Cobra-Goddess!
This is my heart that beats, O Gods,
it rends the horizons of the vault at my forthcoming!
These are my eyes you see, O Gods,
they open up the East and the West
with their wholesome gaze!
These are my nostrils you inhale, O Gods,
they approach with the northern wind as their gale!
These are my two lips that speak, O Gods,
their language fills your ears as the Sun-God's command!
These are my powers you recognize, O Gods,
they precede me in the darkness of the nether vault,
becoming my entourage when I cross
the threshold of the hallowed West!

You know my whisper, my breath,
and the beating of my heart.
You feel my fingers, my toes,
and the skin I had from my Mother.
For she is your Mother too,
and her skin is upon your very bones this day!

I depart from the doorways of this world,
carrying the consolation of things known only to the Gods.
A master of my own flesh,
my flesh is the language of the hallowed.
A master above the sky,
my sky is the sanctuary of the Sun.
A master of the breath in my lungs,
my breath contains the words of deities.
A master of the beating of my heart,
my heartbeat sounds the memory
of the Gods from the ancient beginning.
For I am now a body of radiant light,
in that place they call the hallowed West,
where the Sun-God comes in his old age
to meet the mouth of His Mother.

25: My Eyes Behold An Effective Spirit

Whose words now ring in my ears
upon leaving this western land?
It is the language of the Gods
that becomes my enchantment,
removing the Earth resting heavy on my limbs,
this Earth into whom men retreat
when their time on the banks has ended.
What I have accomplished is the swallowing
of slumber by the nether sky.
She has devoured my sleep,
and fashioned for me the body of a star.
Sky, my Mother, has shouted for me
my inheritance from the stars,
which have risen on the ladder of the East,
making love to the morning horizon.

Departing now, this land of the West
fed by its stream, clad in the shades of its Gods,
and recognized as one of its effective spirits,
I withdraw in the company of the Sun,
His body feeding the mouths of the hungry spirits with gold,
His eyes restoring their sight with beams of turquoise,
His form brightening their twilight waters
with His burnished reflection.
Whose reflection do my eyes see in the water below?
My own two eyes stare back
through the opaque keep of the flood,
and this brilliant countenance is my own,
by whom the spirits are roused.

"Let us remember the language
of that ancient Earth," they say,
"He having come before the primordial Gods;
He having moved the waters, pushing aside their torrent
to stand on the Mound of the first horizon;
He having brightened the first horizon with his mirror;
He having opened his two eyes in the hallows of darkness
to find the earth and sky;
He having pulled the Mound of ages
from the embrace of nether sky;
He having clashed with serpents
on the outer limits of the world;
He having brought the world up and out of darkness;
He being our first sun on our first horizon;
He finding his hand in the shadows
and embracing his loins with her savor;
He becoming she,
and they having spoken the language
of the Gods into existence.
Let us remember them with the language of memory,
which clothes the naked earth,
and returns the stars to their sky!"

Whose language becomes my memory of my many ages?
It is my heart traversing these lonely waters with me,
this waterway being the place
where spirits may forget their memory,
wandering in the shadows
and starving for the Sun-God's light.

It is when we have forgotten
the ancient language of the heart
that we lose the radiance of our effective spirit,
alighting not, but taking flight
as an ibis into the western vault.
Ibis, you with your glimmering crest
are the return of my heart to me.
Remembering your transparent beauty,
your gold-dappled plumage,
your light's mantle of many colors,
I call you to my breast and hold you there.
Your language is the memory of my heart,
speaking from your most ancient time
as the passage of my many ages.

Ibis, who like Moon's crest shines by night,
fills my breast with his awareness light.
I behold the sights that he has seen,
in West's full shadows and East's bright sheen.

My heart flies fast to its ancient source,
upon whose leaves reads a stellar course,
the tree of Gods where the Sun is reborn,
to grapple night's serpent whose coils are shorn.

O Earth of my Father and Mother's sky,
I drink from your tree of my ages gone by,
its waters to fill me as West's shadows fall,
its life to become me as eastern lights call.

A persea tree flowers after gloaming calls,
with malachite leaves and electrum boughs
reaching Heaven's veil.
It beckons the stars to spell out their courses
upon its oracular leaves,
these being written by knowing hands
whose portents govern ages.
This is the place where my ibis heart has led me,
his wings unfurl the leaves
upon which my names are written.
Twilight's ears have never heard my names,
nor slumber imbibed them.
For only the dawn can read this most ancient language,
carried upon the tongue of the north wind and its stars.
Whose stars are these in their ascent over my northern brow?
They are my many and secret names,
clad in the Sun-God's colors.

Here I come in the entourage of the northern stars,
whose channels through the celestial waters
become my guide.
Following after them,
I behold my body rise from its deep horizon,
enchanting the banks of the earth below.
Behold, you earth and sands of the ravenous desert!
I have risen above your graves,
and your sands do not know me.
Your red land cannot possess my shroud of slumber,
nor your spirits hold my heart from its starry flight!

See me now you snares and clutches of the outer darkness,
for I have transformed my shade to become an ibis
of dazzling crest and plumage!
Whose name do I carry in my bill of hallowed metal?
Lord of the Eight Primordials
is my name when my crest glimmers.
It is the badge of the eight and ancient Gods
who assembled in the flood,
their tongues predicting the following of day after night;
their hands weaving the warp of light
with the weft of shadow;
their loins meeting in the embrace
of void and substance;
their feet treading the Mound
and their hands uplifting the vault;
their right eyes foretelling the Sun
and their left eyes foretelling the Moon;
their north becoming the wind,
and their south becoming the waters;
their serpents biting time and swallowing eternity;
and their language twining the first beginning
as the birth of the Gods.

These are the words that have caused
my ascension in the East,
while the West pays me homage
on the day of my farewell.
Not knowing me to tarry in its sands
or follow after its graves,
I go forth by the uplifted hand of the morning sky.

Come near and hear these secrets of the Hidden Shrine
where my effective spirit has flown,
its scent of heady myrrh precedes the forthcoming of a god,
whose tamarisk feet bestow
the lifespan of the sky to Earth's spirits.
Are you one of those spirits of the Earth with famished lips?
Come then and drink these Mysteries
had from the Ancient Earth,
which lifted up the Mound
at the time of the first beginning.
They became the world's nourishment
when the Gods came into being.

My heart is an ibis with a crest of winking silver,
it carries the pale sky upon its wings of divine strength.
His scent is the myrrh which foretells the footfall of Gods,
hidden in their clouds of heavenly savor.
Their feet know the memories of the Ancient Earth,
whose ages came before the birth of breathing beings.
Their ages came before all breath and its speech,
but their breath is the language
through which speech is known.
The tongue cannot speak it nor the breath know it,
until the heart draws it from the Mount of its beginning.
Will you rise as I have risen upon that dawning Mound?

My heart has woven a miracle for my breath and tongue,
proclaiming the speech of the Gods
known before the world's beginning.
These are the words secreted within
the courses of unwearying stars,
the northern and eastern heavens
resounding with their powers.
These are the words that ring in my ears
upon entering this eastern land,
they are the enchantments of the Gods
beheld by my effective spirit.

26: I Go Forth as a Jabiru

This is my going forth predicted by the Sun-God,
He who ascends from the fissure of His mother,
what I have heard chanted by the baboons who greet
the ever-rising countenance of the Sky-Lord,
what my two ears have been opened to hear,
what my mouth, lips, and tongue have repeated,
what the metal of heaven has brought forth
from my earth at twilight,
these powers of the Nether Sky
woven by the Imperishable Stars.
I have seen them coming forth by day at my side,
these Gods and spirits clad in the flight of sunbeams.

You Gods who fill the Earth and Sky,
you spirits whose wings span the two horizons,
and you travelers upon the winds,
I take your direction coming from the North.
Rising like a star of unwearying light,
I become a flashing torch in the presence of the East.
The shades of the Earth behold my luminous face.
With full and open eyes I bequeath them the gift of sight,
and they who were without sight suddenly behold.

It is a wonder to cross the threshold of Gods,
and this I accomplish in the form of a god.
With dappled plumage and a crest of blazing gold,
my lapis lazuli dazzles their eyes, and my turquoise shines
with beams entwined with the raiment of the Sun.

Who calls my name there, opening up the East for my flight?
It is the Unwearying Stars who know my names
and pronounce the savor of a god at my approach,
not with the stride of a human,
but with the lofty stroke of a bird.

I go forth by daybreak as a jabiru of effective light,
being diffused across that eastern horizon,
where the mirror of the sky reigns over millions.
How far my mantle of pure gold is spread,
the span of my wings encompassing the far-traveling clouds.
Blue of lapis, green of turquoise, and fiery red of jasper,
I lay claim to your brilliant enchantments,
carrying these upon the crest of my wings
where come the distant spirits of the sky.

Who makes flight with me
when I open the gates of the North?
It is the circumpolar stars whose faces endure for me,
whose bodies of light appear for the beating of my wings.
They manifest as indestructible gold in my heaven of lapis,
where dwell the Ancestral Souls,
whose torches burn unceasingly.

Approach, come near and open your eyes for me,
you Imperishables of millions of years.
For I am the son of the sky whose endurance is with him,
before whose starry tread impotence flees and death is rent.
Behold with your wholesome eyes my plumage of white light.
See how it glistens in the waters of the sky,
my feet of carnelian beneath me,
and my throat of red jasper upon me.

I have brought with me the mantle of the two horizons,
they are thrown wide open for me at dawn and at eventide,
where their doors of electrum
kiss the tips of my unsullied wings.

I have seen the western vault dance beneath my flight.
She has opened her mouth of starlight
to proclaim me to hidden doors,
where the river is swallowed whole by the shade of the sky;
where her spirits convene as jabirus in her retinue of stars;
where her gap takes Elder Light
within the hallows of the Netherworld;
where the dead come to this place
of the hauling for their reckoning of years;
where the bleariness of the Sacred Eye
is healed within its Mound;
where come the Star-Gods to revive the corpse of the Sun;
where sing the Star-Goddesses
to open the course of the eastern land;
where brightens the world from its kernel of darkness;
where are remembered the divine words
through which the world is reborn.

For I have seen the time of the flood with my two eyes,
and I have beheld the ascension of the Gods to their Mound.
Its earth became the resting place of the Sun,
and its apex the going forth of the eternal sky.
With darkness beneath the face of the Mound,
the world of water was divided in its time,
and this was the first beginning of the Gods,
who have possessed creation
before dark and light were twined.

Their water is still upon them in the West,
where all souls take flight as jabirus
of light-dappled mantles.
And these are my souls,
and these my mantles of radiant savor.

This is my going forth as a soul of infinite life.
I go forth as a jabiru upon unceasing winds.
The sacred eyes of the sky are filled with my splendors,
when I go forth as a jabiru to claim my millions of years.

27: *The Gods Drink Their Image*

I go in carrying my corpse in my hands,
all that I have from my Mother of my many lives,
their fears and transgressions pecking like crows.
These, my entourage from my many lives,
their black cloaks haunting my shade for all its deeds.
We carry with us the corpses of all our accomplishments,
and like sparrows they gossip our names to the sky.
Sky, hungry sky, swallowing my sun into the hallowed West.
You swallow my mortal flesh whole, and with it my deeds,
for the sky is our beginning and our end.
And the Gods drink their image, when it comes back to them.

I go in carrying my fear on my naked bones.
Does he know his name, his scent, his flavor,
all that he has from his Father of his many forms?
Once I was green and gold like a field of corn,
my lighthearted soul fluttering above me as the azure sky.
I knew laughing and drinking and lovemaking,
the gleaming mirror of the sun throbbing from my loins.
I knew the names of my light-spirits, swallows on the wind,
tittering with the sky in the language of the fresh earth,
their speech the ancient tongue of an earth and sky united.
I knew these words and this language in my heart,
which received the knowledge of memory from the swallows,
and they received it from the Sun-God,
whose lotus breath knows our beginning and our end.
And the Gods drink their image, when it comes back to them.

Where are my swallows now,
who saw with their carnelian eyes
the rising of my sun on the fresh horizon of the East
when I was still young,
flawless, and green as the Earth was green;
when I stood with my bare ankles in the flood,
my hands sifting the droplets of their beginning;
when my brow wore the diadem of the Sun's rosy light,
his rays playing over my wet breast and thighs;
when my shade traveled near me
and knew innocence as its companion,
before it played with snares and became entangled in nets;
when my eyes could see the future of their Earth,
his Father below and his Mother above;
when the indomitable mountains appeared yielding
to the soft touch of the eyes, their peaks as lips to kiss;
when my mouth knew its first kiss
and tasted its first lovemaking,
the flood sliding between my open thighs
to receive the power of the desirous Sun;
when my passions knew only their beginning,
never their end?
And the Gods drink their image, when it comes back to them.

My light-spirits began as swallows, as all spirits do,
they know from their birth the language of the rising Sun.
They alight on the edge of the sky to hear the stars,
to catch their unwearying travels
in the words their memory weaves.
This is the language of the swallows kept by the Sun-God,
whose beams traverse the four directions where swallows fly.

Their breasts and rosy faces
have been kissed by the Sun's lips,
and their wings by the midnight sky,
where their flights have ended.

If we spoke the language of swallows,
we would hear how we began,
how the shade of our beginning was fashioned in the deep,
where the coils of serpents choked
the first Mound of the Earth;
how the Sun-God found his mirror
alone in the surging darkness,
peering for the first time
at his reflection of burnished gold;
how the loins of our first Father
grew a sycamore on the Mound,
its boughs the bearers of his passions
stretching from the abyss;
how the turquoise sky was upraised
by the sycamore of the first dawn,
Her body of gold becoming
the Mother of the untiring stars;
how the light-spirits were born as swallows,
to perch near the elder sun,
their ears hearing his first words
ring out into the burden of shadows;
how the bodies of the Gods were fashioned
from the ancient elements,
their powers of gold and turquoise
springing up from the first Mound,
these powers knowing their beginning, but never their end.
And the Gods drink their image, when it comes back to them.

This is where we gathered our powers and our forms,
our lives reaching out before us like shoots of green in a void,
where we began as light-spirits
untarnished by the shade of mortality.
This is how I began when I was still a child and could hear
the language of swallows carried on the wind.
They gave me the memories of the Gods in their first bodies,
which appeared upon the mirror
of waters the beginning held.
Our beginning, our youth,
our green souls were reflected with them.
Many in number, they opened their wet ears
to hear the song of those Gods,
being our gods and our voices, our language and our forms.
How those waters of the void fell from us,
leaving our corpses awake.
How I held my swallows in my hands
like the beatings of my own heart.
Have I now wings to travel
like those hearts on blue-black wings,
to carry words of turquoise
that sprout from stagnant shade?
Have I now wings that know their beginning,
but never know their end?
And the Gods drink their image, when it comes back to them.

I have gone in carrying my heart in my hands,
all that I have from my Mother of my many lives,
and all my Father gave me from his loins clothed in shade.
All my transgressions perch on my heart's shoulders,
like those swallows on sky's edge.

She recalls their exploits as they recall my deeds,
and as the Sun-God knows his language
from beginning's form.
My youth has slumbered within my bones,
my greenest hours faded,
I come again into the breast of the sky
to shed my earthly skin.

Sky, my fragile youth and my beginning,
the Mother of my light-spirit
whose breathing lights the vault,
I drink you in as my lips swallow your starry breast,
your thighs beneath me open
to receive the sun of my green loins.
May my image grow within you as a star of undying aura,
born again in the East on your horizon of ascending light,
this light that glitters by day
in the company of ancient swallows,
reaching up into the turquoise veily
with their lapis wings.

Earth, my heady passions and my forthcoming,
the Father of my flesh and bones,
whose breathing fills the sky,
I drink your seed in as my lips swallow your inundation,
your skin on my skin bestowing me your savor.
May my flesh and bones be received by your hallows
to charge the cavern of beginnings,
where our Ancestors meet to receive their light-spirits
after travels through the memory of time.

Let me travel with them and hear their memories,
to become a swallow of the sky and air
these qualities that know their beginning,
but never their end.
And the Gods drink their image, when it comes back to them.

I go in carrying my peace on sun-clad bones.
He knows his names, his youth, his beginning
all that he has from his Father of his many forms.
He has drunk from his Mother's sky of many lifetimes,
reckoning his past and his many transgressions.
But fear is unknown to him when he passes over
into the house of the midnight sky.
For he has tasted the waters of our beginning,
where all that once was has received the untarnished flood.
His reflection is the green and gold of the untouched Gods,
these qualities knowing their beginning, never their end.
And the Gods drink their image, when it comes back to them.

28: *Where All Spirits Travel*

When my spirit journeys, he crosses the vigorous banks,
to where the mountains command the passing ages.
I take to these western sands with my open mouth,
breathing the taste of years the Gods have reckoned.
Have you counted my years you Gods of the vast regions?
My wings fan out before you as souls to be counted,
here in the land where the ancient earth burns.
And this is where all spirits travel when their time is woven.

I have with me my heart upon my wingspan.
How heavy he can be with the words I have swallowed,
his secrets and his transgressions
written plainly in his vessels.
Will he be silent in the cavern of judges to which he flies,
or will his discontent ring in the ears of the hungry gods?
Your time will not devour me,
you ages I have so greedily consumed,
from the moment of my birth,
thirsting to drink the Sun's green light.
His turquoise knows my longing and kisses my silver bones.
He places his flesh of gold upon me,
in the company of those revered mountains,
for which I spread my wings
and steel my tempestuous heart.
And this is where all spirits travel when their time is woven.

"Open doors for me in the sky as you do for the swallows!"
This is what the half-moon lips
of my heart whisper to the gales.
They seek to wrest my determined flight from me,
their demons meeting my open eyes
with gates closed firm against me.
But I am the luminescence of the Milky Way
brightening the veil.
She takes my seed between golden thighs,
and gives me her lotus breath.
It is her mouth that is open against you,
gales and demons of the celestial keep.
For she is my sky-goddess of forthcoming power,
whose outstretched arms are boundless before me.
Take me in the starry enchantments
of your mouth, O Goddess,
and let the lotus of your lower body unfurl
to give me birth as the rising Sun.
And this is where all spirits travel when their time is woven.

Earth is my memory beneath my beating wings,
its green banks of fleeting glory dancing ever westward.
His body clothed me when he was my ancient father,
his two lips dressed me with words of magical power,
twining the blue and the green of knowledge
about my bare limbs.
I came naked to his mountains and unknowing to his river,
but these he gave to me from his full and open hands.
"Drink," he said, "and know my memories of your beginning,
where blood and seed mingle with flesh and spirit."
How I took what the Earth gave me,
and consumed every element in my heart's path.
And this is where all spirits travel when their time is woven.

I arrived from the East when I was young,
and my turquoise breath became me.
So many mouths kissed that breath,
when the Sun rose fresh on my lips.
Unashamed, I have taken many lovers
to my bed of red jasper,
so like my heart aflame
with the crest of that celestial heron.
He ravishes the naked sky,
where gods and constellations take him,
his rising over the eastern horizon
making lovers of the stars.
But will I find my Earth again,
and will I taste his waters?
The youth inside my heart requires
that flood of blue and green.
Earth and youth are memories
my beating wings carry.
And this is where all spirits travel when their time is woven.

Open doors for me on the Earth as you do for the tamarisk,
in whose green jasper boughs the cheek of the sky is rested.
This is what my open lips desire
as they depart the banks of the living.
How light the touch of those tamarisk branches
upon my unveiled heart,
whose thirsty vessels have known
the flood of that starry goddess.
Her feet received my pilgrimage,
when my famished tongue made prayers,
my throat revived by her watery breast
of Earth and Sky in union.

Your tamarisk is my mother, O veil of light and shade,
over which the swallows travel by daybreak's virgin rays.
These are the rays that become my wings
when I tire in my flight,
when the western gales seal shut
the doors of their impassable sky.
But I pass through on my heron's wings
like sunbeams piercing water,
bursting open the heavenly doors
with arrows of fiery plumage.
These are the beams that know
the mansion of the indestructible stars.
And this is where all spirits travel when their time is woven.

Bring me back to those banks of shooting turquoise
my youth knew with fresh lips and eyes,
where the mountains of ages loomed only at a distance,
but what stretched before me were all my verdant years.
I take these green years in my open mouth,
drinking the ages the Gods have reckoned.
Have you counted my years you Gods of the vast regions?
My heart flies before you as a soul to be born,
here in the land where the ancient sky opens.
And this is where all spirits travel when their time is woven.

29: In the Field of Offerings
The Gods Have Reared Upon Their Words

Clothed in white, my spirit sails the new horizon,
where memory has never been forgotten,
in the place where the face of the northern sky
blushes with stars.
Theirs are remembrances of the first words ever spoken,
heard now with my ears
upon the gusts that celebrate the sunrise.
"You remember where you sailed from,"
they whisper behind my damp ears,
"from that lofty sycamore of memory,
which stretched the womb of the Sky.
She yawned for you with her mouth in the evening,
and took you in with Her flood to ride
the waters where the Sun descends.
The Sun is your companion, like memory,
which rises and falls throughout the ages.
But the knowledge He imparts is the eternal becoming,
which governs all things
the Gods have reared upon their words.

"Gods are this forthcoming with the Sun,
imbibing His memories as beams of light,
then rearing them as language
in the turquoise boughs of the sycamore.
Her branches are the ages
and her leaves every name ever spoken.
Yours are reckoned with their malachite and green of jasper,
their turquoise of the sky,
whose constellations spell out your knowledge.

You have heard this knowledge where you sailed from,
the thighs of your Mother in the East,
which bestowed you your beginning.
Listen to your Mother who resides in the East,
for Hers are the lips that know the memories of the Sun
in His millions of circuits through Her womb,
She who has counted them
and knows their vast enchantments.
How many circuits and how many cycles
has your spirit reckoned?
Look to the stars traversing their river in the sky,
in whose sacred depths the words
of memory remain forever."

I take my oar in hand across the waters,
their azure fills my eyes with the sky,
my heart with the depths.
Gazing up to meet my Mother with fresh eyes and wet ears,
I inhale the savor of this Field of Reeds
in which spirits paddle
the boats of yesterday and tomorrow.
Yesterday I was a sapling of that ancient sycamore,
with no more leaves than days stretching back behind me.
I did not know history or regret, nor the ages of my life,
guided by the Sun's countless risings and settings,
these the courses of nature which remained a mystery
to my untested countenance.

Mother, take me to your holy shore
from my boat of offerings.
Let me offer what I bring to the Sky who bore me,
feeding me Her breast
from which my names of many ages fell.

Let me offer my feet to the Earth who carried me,
giving me his roads and his fields of verdant memory.
Let me offer my legs to the mountains who stood for me,
enduring my deeds as I traversed my name of history.
Let me offer my knees to the trees who bent for me,
showing my body the ladder ascended by spirits.
Let me offer my loins to the fields who gave me their seed,
sprouting for me the numberless
beginnings of which we are made.
Let me offer my manhood to the vault's unwearying stars,
ascending for me as a map
of my becoming in the twilight sky.
Let me offer my navel to the sacred river who brought me,
quenching my ignorance
with the flood of our ancient memory.
Let me offer my breast to the South who nourished me,
bringing me the waters
beneath which my memory was renewed.
Let me offer my throat to the North who breathed me,
exhaling the divine language through which I live again.
Let me offer my mouth to the West who took in my corpse,
weaving for me a pristine form
from the net of indestructible stars.
Let me offer my eyes to the East who beholds the reborn sun,
seeing my spirit come forth by dawn
as a swallow of bright light.
Let me offer my nostrils to the wind who brought me
forward,
urging my bones to know their own strength against the tide.
Let me offer my ears to the swallows
who carry the voice of the Gods,
reminding my heart who truly gave
its beating and its breath.

Let me offer my brow to the peaks
which pierce the veil of heaven,
bestowing my two eyes sight
of the doors through which spirits fly.
Let me offer the vessel of my heart
to the Gods who comprise creation,
holding all the worlds in their tongues of sacred memory.

Mother, lead me to the waters of the sky
where the stars never rest.
May they receive with their radiant hands my offerings,
my bones and my flesh clad in a pure mantle of light.
See my open palms raised to the starry vault above my brow,
and shine with your voice the knowledge
of the open sky where I sail.
For I am your secret son
born from the gap in the eastern sky,
and what I know is what throws wide open
the doors of the portal of light.
I have seen by the renewed flame of the Sun
that heron of flashing plume,
whose crest has become my crest
on the golden thighs of dawn.
His language is my language which bespeaks the Gods,
numberless as the unceasing stars in the midnight sky.
She is my sky and my Mother,
lifting me up by her flood to the place of my new beginning.

I take my oar in hand to the horizon
where spirits rise as herons.
They alight for my outstretched arms
on their Mound of our beginning.
Remove the earth from my well-traveled feet
and give me my birth from this Mound
where the flood retreated from the Sun.
I come clothed in white to drink the ancient waters.
This is the treading-place of spirits on their celestial wings,
where I too have traveled in a boat,
sped by the arms of Mother Sky.
She yawned for me with Her mouth in the morning,
opening Her horizon to send me forth where the Sun ascends.
The Sun is my companion, like memory,
which enters and departs throughout my ages,
but the knowledge He imparts is my eternal becoming,
which governs all my forms
the Gods have reared upon their words.

30: We Are All Shadows
Traveling Through the Open Doors

Earth, you are the residence of my bones,
the keep of my flesh with me from the beginning,
the house my ancient father made for me.
I will never be separated from you,
as your mountains will never be
separated from your horizons.
They will endure on your loins as the sycamore endures,
rearing the green essence of field and meadow,
orchard and vineyard, cavern and grove.
You have passed to me these secret things from your seed,
and I carry them with me as the swallows carry the Sun.

Sky, you are the residence of my spirit,
the keep of my shade with me from the beginning,
the house my ancient mother made for me.
I will never be separated from you,
as your stars will never be separated from your vault.
They will remain imperishable
as your directions are imperishable,
holding aloft the gleam of Mooring Post and Bull's Foreleg,
She-Hippopotamus and Crocodile, Lion and Myriad.
You have passed to me
these constant things from your breast,
and I carry them with me
as the winds carry the clouds.

We are all shadows
traveling through the open doors of the Earth,
who gives us His seed of the ages
stretching back to our beginning,
where we come from the gap of darkness and into the day;
where the thighs of our mother
stretch forth to give us the world;
where the world is held up by the ocean encircled by void;
where the void is the source of the many
from which the world is woven;
where darkness is the warp
and light the weft of the primordial gods;
where the Gods comprise earth and sky,
below and above, seed and womb;
where are hidden the children of the earth
in the tears of daylight;
where the West swallows the stars
that are born again from her body;
where the East spreads wide
for the mirror of the swelling Sun;
where are completed all the Mysteries
that go forth as creation's shadows.

We are all shadows
traveling through the open doors of the Sky,
who gives us her breast
of the eternal courses traversed by the Sun,
traversed by the Unwearying Stars who rise and set by me;
traversed by the ark of daybreak which sails with me;
traversed by the ark of twilight which moors with me;
traversed by the souls of the North,
which provide breath for me;

traversed by the souls of the South,
which provide water for me;
traversed by the hawk of the East, who shines gold on me;
traversed by the stork of the West, who gives flight to me;
traversed by the Sun-God, whose right eye opens for me;
traversed by the Moon-God, whose left eye opens for me;
traversed by all the Secrets that go forth as life's shadows.

We are all shadows
traveling through the open doors of flesh and bone.
I take the pathway of doors my corpse provides,
steering me with the hand of my senses into the field beyond.
Life is my father, the deeds of my skin,
and death is my mother,
whose clothing of the dusk conceals the virgin dawn.

We are all shadows
traveling through the open doors of the eyes.
I take the road of doors my mirrors provide,
gazing through my corpse
and predicting the spirit following the flesh.
Daylight is the map my living feet tread,
and nightfall is the guide of my starry stride.

We are all shadows
traveling through the open doors of the ears.
I take the counsel of doors my music provides,
singing from the sparrows who hear the Sun's summons.
Earthly voices are the direction of my bones,
while the words of the Sky provide wings for my soul.

We are all shadows
traveling through the open doors of the nose.
I inhale the incense of doors the Earth provides,
swelling my worldly lungs
with the savor of the immortal Gods.
Sweat is the scent of my corpse of the Earth,
while breath is the flavor of my spirit of air going forth.

We are all shadows
traveling through the open doors of the mountains.
I ascend the soil of doors the beginning provides,
bursting up through the ocean of my mother as the mound.
My base is the road taken by the Sun when He declines,
while my apex is the golden throne His ascension mounts.

We are all shadows
traveling through the open doors of the winds.
I sail the watercourse of doors sky's breath provides,
moving in and moving out from the reach of the horizons.
My coming from the North revivifies the eternal sky,
while my coming from the South renews the enduring Earth.

We are all shadows
traveling through the open doors of the rivers.
I quicken the flood of doors the netherworld provides,
overflowing every channel
where my name spreads like water.
My water of the fields is the green of precious turquoise,
while my water in the sky is the starry veil of lapis lazuli.

We are all shadows
traveling through the open doors of the East.
I take to my breast the lotus of doors daybreak provides,
striking my heart with the fiery crest of a heron.
His call is my name rising from the pyramidion of the Sun,
and his alighting is my soul's forthcoming
to the region of eternity.

We are all shadows
traveling through the open doors of the West.
I enter the mouth of doors twilight provides,
reuniting with my Mother who acclaims Her star-born child.
Her darkness is the secret cavern
where my corpse is renewed,
while Her light is the celestial door thrown open for my soul.

I am a shadow, like all the shadows
traveling through the open doors of the worlds.
We enter the lifetimes of doors eternity provides,
going forth by dawn and coming in by dusk.
Our life is the earth our corpse mirrors in daylight,
while death is the sky our soul ascends when night is opened.

31: I Know the Language of Swallows

The Sky is my mother who summons me from the West,
her net of gods shining over her body of stellar metal,
they who appear upon her mantle of lapis lazuli,
glimmering over the horizon as dust of fine gold.
I came forth from her when the fresh East yawned,
passing the morning beetle of iridescent shell and wing.
How I made my youthful appearance over these lands,
bolstered by the north wind whose voice knows my name.

This wind-god says to me,
"My Sky-Goddess calls you in the West.
She holds the gate of the hidden land
in Her mouth of the Unwearying Stars,
where fly the bird-souls who converse with the Sun.
Behold their ruddy faces and wings of burnished metal,
going round the limits of the sky who speaks their tongue,
the language of the East which howls with the dawn,
which declares life and denies slumber.

"I soar beneath the bellies of the clouds that uplift swallows,
who in their beaks carry the words
of the Sun-God when he sails.
They rise by me to declare what they know,
and you rise by me.
What you know is that eastern tongue
which reckons the dawn,
its light-rays and heron of dazzling white crest.
My eyes are open and rise as the heron rises.
You too with open eyes shall rise as the heron rises,
with crest of curd white and mantle of blinding electrum.

"You enter the West as a ram of the Earth with aged skin,
with dusky gold as your flesh and silver as your bones.
When the swallows titter to my clouds,
they tell of your sleep,
what all mortals come to,
when they walk in the East and veer west,
when they draw the breath of sky and eat from the Earth.
But the West knows the East as South foretells North,
and your feet of these directions
follows your breath of the sky."

My breath is my mother who embraces me in the North.
she appears to set me upright between her rosy-gold thighs,
the ladder where souls burst forth to herald eternity.
I am fashioned from their same metal,
from their mirror of electrum.
When I appear it is with the face of the untarnished sun,
rising as the Wind-God said I would,
cognizant of the language of swallows.

Do living beings know the language of swallows?
We see them weave to and fro in the boughs of the sycamore,
our eyes of Earth blind against
the train of spirits rising with them.
For their eyes are of spirit while their wings alight on Earth,
unlike the eyes of mortals
which see only earth and know only skin.
But I who know the Sun-God take up His colors on my flesh,
and when I go into the West
it is with the wings of a dawn-knowing swallow.

You swallows of the Sun-God bear
His holy marks on face and breast.
Red is the Sun-God's color
when He rises with your sanguine wings,
when He captures the eastern sky from its nighttime coils.
My face glows red and my breast is dappled with jasper,
having gazed upon your sycamores
and made my flight between them.
Your wings know my arms, you swallows,
and your red cowl becomes me.
It brightens the pre-dawn horizon
with the blood of my enemies,
sleep in the West and bleariness in my eyes.
These eyes of mine are open with the eyes of swallows,
never bleary, and sharp with the lance of first light.

These swallows say to me,
"Look! Open your eyes to see
the thighs of your mother opening.
She is the lamp of the nether sky,
uplifting the lamps of the stars to Her breasts,
these gods of the primordial sea,
who light the way for spirits traveling.
Travel then, when your time for entering the West comes!
Travel with our wings upon you
so that your feet do not tarry on the Earth,
but they mix with the Unwearying Stars that sweep the East,
that drive forward the clouds and herald the day.

"Our enchantments are the East which meets birth,
the Earth that meets Sky;
the gap of the West that meets bird-souls;
the breath that meets the North;
the flood that meets the South;
the turquoise that meets the desert;
the date palm that meets the arid country;
the acacia that meets the rain;
the lotus which meets the nose of the Sun;
the Sun who meets the horizon;
the horizon which meets the nether sky;
the nether sky which meets the earth above.

"These are the enchantments, the words,
the language the Sun-God tells us.
And only the ears that hear His colors may know His speech.
They who know His colors, and thus know His speech,
will know the lives He lives.
His colors are these Gods upon Him,
which see His lives as theirs in the sky.
So know his colors and thus his lives,
and live as he lives in the eternal sky!"

The sky is my mother who raises me in the East,
her skin of brilliant fabric woven from the stars,
they whose unwearying eyes see spirits rise
as swallows of the ruddy dawn.
I came forth from her with their language on my lips,
open with the lance of daybreak by which the Earth lives.
This is how I live again, once the West has summoned,
when my tread follows birds of iridescent crest and wing.
How I make my youthful appearance over these lands,
uplifted by the North Wind whose voice knows my name.

32: Raise Up My Body
Let Your Sky Receive Me

My journey has brought me across the horizons
where sparrows carry the tongue of the Sun-God.
His words of dusk and daybreak
shatter the loneliness of the sky,
now bright, now forlorn as morning and evening seek me.
What have I to do with sparrows who gossip of nightfall,
who summon with their little wings
the movements of the veil?
I listen, and they speak of the Sun-God's fragile skin,
a pale lotus of celestial blue.
He rises for them to unfurl His divine petals,
the language of the sky,
whereupon they chatter the words
that part the veil before them.

Have they come to twitter of my slumber,
these sparrows who carry the mark of fire upon their breast?
I would be warmed by the face of their Sun,
not drowned in the waters beneath the Earth,
nor taken down by the cavern
where wings tread the darkness.
The Earth has become my father again,
as He was when I was His seed.
Shall I become a field of turquoise glimmering,
or a pasture of malachite summoning the flood?
If the Earth is my father,
then I shall wear a crown of cypress
upon my dusky brow.
I shall call the willow my second home,
its mournful boughs my refuge.

I would have the bright wings of a heron,
whose immaculate sheen recalls the Sun-God's first morning,
that morning which came fast over the torrent of the abyss,
pushing from it the sacral mound of the first beginning.
Here I would take the hand of my mother
stretching out from the stars.
She comes from the Unwearying Ones.
She comes from the North,
where rise but never tarry the Ancients who flew before me.
Mother, I see your starry breast
and seize your glinting fingers.
Your metal is gold which I take to my lips.
Your breast, a constellation.
These are the stars that carry me
to your thighs where life is waiting.

The heights I was called down from
have called me back again.
The Earth who is my keeper must give way to Heaven's gaze.
The Bull's Thigh who bore me now appears before my eyes,
in whose lofty reflection the North
is roused from its western daze.
Who comes in the North to be my mother,
who opens wide her thighs,
my yawning horizon of eastern metal
with electrum in her eyes?

You goddess of northern breast and eastern thighs,
where the Sun-God travels to recover his face of morning,
open for me your cleft of the dawn
and secure for me our beginning.
I approach with the flesh and bones of a mortal man.
Raise up my body from the Earth
and let your sky receive me!
I approach with the bleary eyes of a twilight wanderer.
Open wide my eyes with northern light
and let your stars behold me!
I approach with lips sealed fast by the nether sky.
Open up my mouth with heavenly metal
and let your speech become me!
I approach with nostrils shut against the wind.
Open up my nose with that heavenly lotus
and let your breath suffuse me!
I approach with loins of western slumber.
Open up my channels with living blood
and let your womb conceive me!
I approach with the sand of the desert on my feet.
Open up the river above my brow
and let your flood cleanse me!
I approach knowing the season of nightfall.
Open up the day before my feet
and let your dawn shine through me!

I see the sparrows now and hear their language in my heart,
not the gossip of the evening, but the words of the morning,
ringing clear through the passing clouds.
They pass on by, but I do not pass,
with lips and nostrils breathing.
My heart has sheltered a heron,
who knows what the great Gods know.
The Earth that gives us cannot keep us,
like the mountains that kiss the Sky.
Our Earth becomes our Father,
but our Mother lifts us high.

Father, I have my bones from you,
my skin and breath of clouds.
But these things I return to you
when the heights call me back to her arms.
I hear the willow and cypress,
the boughs of your ancient sycamore.
But he too lets go of my feet
when the tread of the sky finds my toes.
My arms become the wings of a heron
to know the Imperishable Stars.
And I like they have a crest for a mirror,
from which the Sun-God shines.

Mother, your body takes my earthly bones,
my skin and eyes of water.
These things began in the heights of your stars
where the light that guides the Earth comes.
I behold your northern sky, your cleft of gold and its ocean.
Blood swells my loins and I enter the lips
where life first hears its calling.
O you goddess of twilight breast and morning thighs,
where all souls travel to recover
their first language of the sky,
open for me your legs of the soul-house
and give me my beginning.
I approach with the flesh and bones of a mortal man,
raise up my body from the earth and let your sky receive me.

33: I Walk With Spirits

I walk with the desert.
He is the red land of my sorrow and regret,
clinging to my feet as the sand of ages past.
He stretches out not as a lover,
but as a debtor demanding recompense.
My sky takes me by the hand in the face of those sands,
and on the distant horizon I behold the mirror of water.
She is the mother of my new life, waiting,
so I have come back to the place where my feet began.

I walk with the trees,
remembering the yew of my boyhood,
whose words of the future heralded my past.
To be reborn through memory,
would be my mountain to climb.
He has boughs of yesterday and leaves of tomorrow,
my yew who keeps our past and remembers our future.
Older than the vault of the sky,
his prophecies hold our beginning.
Through him I recall the breath of myrrh,
the Sacred Ones who travel.
They are the Gods who offered me my lungs,
who gave me the Ancestral breath.
He is the father of my new memory, enduring,
so I have come back to the place where my history began.

I walk with the river.
She rushes over my feet to find me my spirit,
who travels along the watery road
where life and death mingle.

Has she swallowed the crocodiles that wait in the darkness,
my pains of sharp teeth who surface to remind me?
Or has she drowned them,
those sorrows of impenetrable scales,
my boyhood and wayward youth who hunger to surface?
But I will not find them,
not in the shallows where the lotus rises.
He pushes up his face from the mud to drink the golden light.
This is what spirits do when they find darkness,
and this is what my spirit becomes
when first light catches his eyes.
He is the lotus that came from my beginning, opening,
so I have come back to where my spirit began.

I walk with my body,
who carries the scars of my mother and father upon him.
For we all wear our history like clothes,
putting some on with relish and discarding others.
How my wardrobe has ransomed my heart
for their promises.
I had the scarf of youth and the boots of pleasure,
now worn out like my hands,
who carry my heart in thin fingers.
I will not now count the brilliant fabrics I possessed,
now that my body moves sky-clad beneath a mantle of stars.
For this is where I came from,
and where you who read me were born.
My stars take me by the fingers and lead me to sky's shelter.
She is the lapis womb whose waters receive me, swimming,
so I have come back to where my flesh began.

I walk with my lovers,
they give me their manhood and mine,
their skin and consolation.
I have had them by moonlight,
where my lips taste ivory beams.
I have had them by daybreak,
where the Sun strikes naked thighs with gold.
I have heard the promises of sages warning of the flesh.
Where are their bones now?
I have listened to the sacral threats of ages.
Have their fears ever shown us how?
Now I take you with me, all you lovers from my bed.
In memory you live again, on lips and breath and kisses.
You have taught me how precious a gift life is
shorter than twilight,
and sweeter than vain promises or threats.
You are the thighs my spirit enters, renewing,
so I have come back to where my heart began.

I walk with my heart, gleaming even after nightfall
as a stone of sanguine carnelian.
He holds the Sun between his lips even after sundown.
He has been lost in a bramble where my hopes found him,
as all hearts are found even when shade takes them.
Shade, you are a gale in the hands of time,
but you make the heart endure with its fragile light.
It is light that bends like a sapling,
yet withstands the gale of experience.
Now I imbibe the wind at my back,
tasting what life has given me.
And it is still life as it pours from one vessel to another.
He is the container of the Sun in which I set, rising,
so I have come back to where my light began.

I walk with swallows,
those little birds of great flight who soar over seas,
their untiring wings find me wherever I wander.
Give me your cloaks of lapis lazuli, your hood of blood red,
and give me your morning call to summon the potent sun.
Yours is the language of time's beginning
where mortals are made.
Yours is sight of sunbeams upheld by wings of shade.
I open my body to let my spirit fly with you.
And this is where we all travel once our skins are shed.
You are the voices of earth that mingle with heaven, flying,
so I have come back to where my speech began.

I walk with the dead.
They came before me with the rising sun,
and they departed when the song of eventide ended.
They are my mothers and my fathers,
my conscience and memory.
I remember we came from many,
no matter how the one howls.
It is the Ancestors who keep me
in the language of their names.
Their names are the warp and weft
from which our future weaves.
I make my heart a libation from which my past drinks,
while my future is a stream of memories,
pouring from history's bones.
I open my memory to let my body become you.
And this is where we multiply once we set our memory free.
You are the ages past from where I hail, living,
so I have come back to where my future began.

I walk with spirits,
who pass through the doors of flesh and bone,
who know where the Earth meets the Sky.
They know the caverns in the ever-standing mountains,
the portals of imperishable stars flashing.
Their river is a road in the nether sky,
where wings of sparrows tread.
They make of the Earth a memory,
and from Sky they make a bed.
How soft their whisper in half-forgotten words,
I hear with open heart.
How our past comes calling when our spirit makes a start.
My shadow takes my fingers and leads me to a door
the Earth becomes my lintel as the Sky becomes my floor.
You are the memory of me time keeps, returning,
so I have come back to where my travels began.

I walk with the Gods.
They came before us with the rising waters,
and They have never departed,
even as our memory faded.
They are our mothers and fathers,
our beginning and our end.
And I remember we came from many,
no matter how the one howls.
You found me when I was naked on the other shore,
your doors in the sky you opened,
where my feet of the Earth could drink.
The desert of my memory becomes a field of turquoise,
where the sycamore and tamarisk hold the florid sky.
I am the memory of leaves and branches
glistening in the green.

Now the sparrows find me as a home for the weary vault.
Come Gods, you stellar wings of Earth and Sky,
lift up my bones of memory,
where stars make bright their doors.
I open up my body to let my memory become You.
And this is where immortality finds us
once we set our memory free.
You are creation's waters where spirits hail, ascending,
so I have come back to where my soul began.

34: Blackbird In the House of Memory

Blackbird came to fetch me
on the day Winter became my lover.
His wings brought the chill of dusk
from a place the Sun could not reach.
"There is always such a place," Blackbird taught me,
"a place where the forlorn shadows of trees
hang heavy across the forbidding mounds,
a place where the Gods of the hearth may not be summoned,
a place where the bones of the dead are eaten,
a place where youth and beauty cannot be remembered.
These things are with you, too," Blackbird said,
on the day he came to fetch me.

To find rain when drought has gained
a foothold at my door;
to find an empty pail full of milk in my pasture;
to hear the oak and the willow exchange memories
of my youth;
to find sparrows trapped in a net and set them free,
these I cherish when Blackbird comes,
to remind me of the Sky's offerings on my behalf.

"Do not come to rue the day you were born,"
Blackbird said, as my skin felt the evening approach.
"Your skin is a house of memory for your lovers,
so let your lovers in.
Do not waste your years on making of your flesh
a graveyard for the passions,
a charnel house where pleasures go to die.

"Take hold of their senses in your naked breast,
and wrap their wings around you.
Swallows and finches flutter to your door,
their beaks carrying the voice of Summer.
But how Winter longs to be your lover
when the arms of the Sun open wide."

I held up the cloak of my lovers,
on the day Blackbird came.
The weave of their kisses and climaxes,
their lips of precious stone,
the fabric of their passions,
hours spent nestled against fur and groin.
The interlacing of forms tasting my eyes,
their sweat and sinews twining my thighs,
without a thought of dusk or winter,
I gave my provisions away.
Lust, love, and virtue seemed a meager price to pay.

"My house of memory is a home inhabited by myriads,"
I said to Blackbird waiting on the earth.
"My flesh too is a vessel from which many have drunk,
many lips from the time I was a boy;
many hands before I knew what they were for;
many loins spilling seed before I knew how;
many bites and many kisses traveling;
many tongues and many words expended;
many twilights caught in a net of promises;
many mornings rising with regrets.
But these are the seeds of a great tree that has grown,
and its leaves are all the memories my skin has known."

Blackbird came to fetch me
on the day forgetfulness became my lover.
His wings brought the hearth of the Gods
which the one from the East had claimed.
"There have always been gods," Blackbird taught me,
"and always a hearth burning,
always the great Sun who shone from the waters;
always the Moon whose silver mirror beckons;
always the dancing stars of untiring guidance;
always the Sky of shifting moods and veils;
always the mountains crowning the horizons;
always the rivers to carry the souls of men.
These things are with you, too," Blackbird said,
on the day he came to fetch me.

To find the sacred fire others said was extinguished;
to hear the language of the Sun from the mouths of swallows;
to see the ancient Gods beaming through Moon's phases;
to dance in accordance with the unwearying stars;
to be clothed in the sky, its lapis and its gold;
to drink the mountain and the river
with open lips and open palms,
these I cherish when Blackbird comes,
to remind me of the Earth's offerings on my behalf.

"Do not come to rue the day you were born,"
Blackbird said, as my heart felt the morning approach.
"Your heart is a house of memory for your Gods,
so let your Gods in.
Do not waste your years on making of your center
a blighted field for the spirit,
a place of desolation where devotion goes to die.

"Take hold of their powers in your naked hands,
and wrap their enchantments around you.
Hawks and ravens make a path to your door,
their feet in unison with the veil above them.
And how the Earth longs to be your lover
when the arms of the Sky open wide."

I held up the torch of my Gods on the day Blackbird came.
The flame of their boons and curses;
their skins of precious metal;
the light of their transformations;
seasons shifting from form to form;
the interweaving fabrics of soul and skin;
their breadth of design without and within;
without a thought of dawn or spring,
I gave my mortality away.
Flesh, blood, and bone seemed a meager price to pay.

"My house of memory is a home
inhabited by a myriad of gods,"
I said to Blackbird waiting in the air.
"My spirit too is a vessel
from which many gods have drunk,
the gods of the nighttime sky, knowing darkness;
the gods of first light, knowing the mortal hours;
the gods of the two horizons,
knowing life and knowing death;
the gods of the western mountains, knowing sleep's breath;
the gods of eastern peaks, waking bleary Earth;
the gods of the nether waters, knowing celestial birth;
all the gods from which immortality is sewn.
But these are the seeds of a great tree that has grown,
and its leaves are all the memories my heart has known."

35: What Do You Hear
I Hear the Gods

What do you hear in that hour they call twilight?
Stars that have overcome the horizon
with cloaks of blue and gold,
who in their luminescent hands hold
the departed spirits of the Earth below.
They reach your ears with messages from the Sky,
opening the doors we enter when we die.
They have for ears and eyes the patterns
of souls rising for the dance,
beheld by the Earth in silent awe.

I hear the Gods who weave their twilight home,
the gold that beckons eyes to horizon's fire,
her breast pointed high to clasp spirit's wings,
they who reach the crimson-painted clouds,
before the darkness finds them to blanket their ascent.
These mysteries show their colors to my eyes,
as I watch for the spirits who come to claim the skies.

What do you hear when the sycamore sways?
The past who in his fingers holds
the lovers who have scratched their names
on your breast of gold,
with a silver mirror to dress your eyes,
and a shadow of copper where your spirit flies.
He is a past of gilded fabric,
whose shimmer rekindles yesterday in his garden
of trees that count your forgotten years,
when dusky soil has taken your flesh and tears.

I hear the Gods who have woven the Earth
by their hands of gold and brow of stars,
who came before the green beneath us grew
with their language of sparrow and Morning Star,
upon whose breezes the waters of beginning stirred.
I find in the mountains the stone and metals of their tongue,
speaking clear to the coming dawn.
She parts her veil for the arousal of those peaks,
whose lips seek a turquoise embrace
from that mouth into which he speaks.

What do you hear when the cornflower opens?
The thread of life calling from the mantle of the dead,
where flesh and bone are buried with a wreath upon his head.
Your lover called youth and time, endless it seems by dawn
standing green with Spring's fair blooms,
until by dusk they are gone.
I knew him to be a swallow on the air
who carried me to pasture, to orchard and home.
This wreath of sky-blue flowers on my brow,
whose beauty like daybreak was destined to roam.

I hear the Gods as they dance in their orchards,
trees of myrrh who commune with the acacia,
of ancient leaves and boughs.
They break open the sky with their ageless stories
with fruit that speaks a stellar tongue.
This language is the memory of many,
before the one came.
She tells the fruit of legions, before his jealous claim.
I read with open eyes and hear with open ears
the music of the sky that reckons
the memory of myriad years.

What do you hear when your soul flies?
Your wings calling the winds their home,
above the place where mountains open their peaks,
where he catches the gaze of the West as it sees,
as the voice of the vault clearly speaks.
Is this where you find your flesh and your bones,
renewed in a western shrine,
where before you have gone the dreams of living beings,
taken as lovers by time.
This place where go the feet of dreams
with lovers on his brow,
we call the thighs of sacred death
before whom our dreams bow.

I hear the Gods in their shrine called memory
from whose breast the ancient tongues are nourished,
with their skies and trees and myriad fields
traversed by the wings of their stellar spirits.
This is where we go when the hour called twilight ripens,
when she reaches out her hand
to take back the dust of her ages.

This is where I go when my flesh tires of bone
and these are the Gods who meet me with gold,
when the dusky veil opens to welcome me home.
I hear with open ears and see with open eyes
the chanting of the fields where death's mantle unravels
I hear with open ears and see with open eyes
the courses of many that govern life's travels,
by whose hands the Earth meets the skies.

36: I Stay With These Gods
My Heart and Hands Have Known

I am with them through the gates,
these Gods that come from the clouds,
these Gods that divide the sky
into regions of North and South.
The North coming down
as the breath I breathe when my mouth is opened,
when they who exhale the clouds
have parted my lips to kiss life,
whereupon the North is my lover,
and the South has flowed up
to dance across my feet.
And I stay with these Gods
my breath and feet have known.

I am with Them through the passage land,
these Gods that speak in the stone and mountains,
these Gods that unite the Earth and Sky
to make a spirit-body in the East and West.
The East being Theirs from which the Sun is born,
where I raise up my solar bones from slumber,
and it is here that my flesh becomes gold.
Glimmer on my skin, you Gods of the dawn,
Who appear on blue waters above and below.
Take my hand into Your reflection,
to pass from the surface and into your realm of light.
Let the West take on my shadow.
And when he comes to cast his shade over the Earth,
let him dance across my thighs again,
and I stay with these Gods
my bones and thighs have known.

I am with them through the rain that falls,
these Gods that catch the Heavens
as they descend to quench their Earth,
these Gods that summon flood and cloud
with names of precious stone.
With all their colors spelled out in the sky,
they echo from cloud to mountain
in a tapestry of light and sound.
They recount for Earth the deeds above him.
This is where I find myself
during that time of star and twilight
on a horizon swimming in the river of the sky,
naked with my heart in my hands.
Read what is written in this fiery vessel,
and you will fill your eyes with stellar deeds
from a secret keep I have veiled with a river,
flooding for those whose fields have been planted.
I spring up with these Gods in the rain,
to dance across the vineyards,
and I stay with these Gods
my heart and hands have known.

I am with them through the flames that spark,
these Gods that make us live again.
They come when light calls them,
when the East and West are ablaze.
And I call them, at first light and nightfall,
to shine with their lips upon my heart's embers.
They will not be held at bay,
by gales or mouths kept silent.
They leap from the world beyond the world,
when the fire of memory is recalled.

My thoughts have a spirit's wings,
my memories a desert wind,
the embers my heart has guarded
will revivify their blazing forms.
I come with them to dance their dance,
these Gods my spark has shown,
and I will stay with these Gods
my voice and flame have known.

37: May the Gods Open A Door

I awake to a life hidden
behind the world's dusky veil.
She finds me as my mother,
rising up between Her loins of celestial metal.
What finds me is our cavern of beginnings,
where swim the wings of souls.
What finds me is our lake in the nether sky,
where fly the shadows charged by Heaven's breast.
May the Gods open a door
for the passage of my solar wings.
May the Gods open a door
for the breath my mother sings.

My eyes tread the courses of the stars,
untiring in their house of North.
In this direction I am taken by them
to the region where horizons gaze,
to behold our bodies glittering
with skins of gold and precious stone.
I am open in the direction of the ever-rising Sun,
with brows of lapis lazuli curving on Heaven's crown.
May the Gods open the sky
for my flesh of stellar design.
May the Gods open the sky
for these shining wings of mine.

It is from the soil I swell with malachite presence,
my naked feet known to the sacral ground below.
He knows my seed of green,
from which His mighty sycamore has grown.

He knows my heady scent of myrrh,
from which His power is sewn.
I now behold green jasper, inhale breath of myrrh,
knowing the seeds of tomorrow, and all the seeds that were.
May the Gods open the Earth
for my feet of stone and seed.
May the Gods open the Earth
for these feet to take their lead.

I have come on voice of Sky,
upon celestial breath.
He recounts the moment of my birth,
His open arms take my death.
He has given His hallows beneath ancient trees,
whose branches foretell my years with seeing leaves.
I come to receive a mantle of stone,
alighting as a swallow in the boughs I call home.
May the Gods open a field,
for my wings as they grow.
May the Gods open a field
for my enchantments that flow.

Now I come to a river of luminous spirit,
spreading the loins of the eastern horizon.
She is a flower in the river of the sky,
opening Her wet petals for my loins as they fly.
She is a mother of gleaming turquoise breast,
holding the Sun tightly in Her woven gold nest.
I am now wet as the day I was born,
reared on milk of Sky, fresh on the breast of Morning.

May the Gods open a lotus,
for my face of youthful power.
May the Gods open a lotus
for my mirror of the dawning hour.

I came from the cleft of my Mother,
from the seed my Father spilled.
Hers is the sacred cavern,
from manhood of Earth being filled.
His are the eyes that see me spring,
at sacred daybreak on His bank.
Hers are the lips the Sun hears sing,
when I ascend Her gilded flank.
May the Gods open a body,
for my wings to take their flight.
May the Gods open a body
for my dawn and star by night.

My skin recalls His bones when Morning comes,
and when night falls he hears the summons of His blood,
these the fragile gifts of Earth,
the sacral river and Her mud.
I swim with the Sky as the East is born,
and by the West I travel as His daylight is shorn.
The feet that move me are of Earth,
of tree and holy peak,
the arms that keep me are of Sky,
the mansion Earth's eyes seek.
May the Gods open a soul,
for these bones to open their way.
May the Gods open a soul
for my coming forth by day.

38: Meeting At the Gates

There is a meeting at the gates
where I walk in the company of the rain.
The sky is written upon his body
as he falls to the thirsty earth below,
my earth that drinks him deeply,
that finds consolation in his lofty messages,
my earth that needs the kisses
of that place behind the veil,
my earth that gathers all the sky sends,
to hold it for my meeting at the gates.

There is a meeting at the gates,
where I dance in the company of the desert.
The wind is written upon his body
as he shifts across his barren kingdom,
my kingdom of the spirit lifted
above the flesh and bones he knows,
my kingdom twined with cliff and stone,
opening for the tips of these etheric wings,
my kingdom of unceasing air,
that holds the spaces for my meeting at the gates.

There is a meeting at the gates,
where I dress in the company of the Sun.
Pure gold is written upon his body
as he travels through the shadowy sky below,
my sky that spreads her body for him,
that receives the tokens of life he gives,
my sky that wears the messages
of those stars above the veil,
my sky that reads the wandering bodies,
and holds their maps for my meeting at the gates.

There is a meeting at the gates,
where I fly in the company of swallows.
Messages of the Sky are written upon their bodies
as they travel to and fro between the worlds,
my worlds of earth and air,
between which the Gods are known,
my worlds within this skin and bones,
growing from my soil like a tree,
my worlds that keep my secret deeds,
until they fly forth for my meeting at the gates.

There is a meeting at the gates,
where I awake in the company of jabirus.
The Gods are written upon their wings
as they break the silence of the twilight hour,
my hour of shattering the dusky veil
rising between my corpse and soul,
my hour of hearing the message of stars,
calling through the doors of that secret world,
my hour of kindling the fire within my bones,
as it lights my way for my meeting at the gates.

There is a meeting at the gates,
where I make love in the company of a heron.
My heart is written upon his gleaming breast
as he rises above me to open my eyes,
my eyes that know the horizons of the sky,
between which the Sun dances his seasons,
my eyes that see the spirits who know me,
riding high on their western peak,
my eyes that foretell the beating of my heart
that holds the rhythm for my meeting at the gates.

There is a meeting at the gates,
where I swim in the company of a sacred lotus.
My future is written upon his sky-blue petals
as he opens in the waters to herald the dawn,
my dawn wearing the embrace of myrrh
as he spreads through the arms of his sky,
my dawn wearing a mantle of fine gold,
predicting midday fire above his watery veil,
my dawn that finds its hidden light shining
beyond the shadows for my meeting at the gates.

There is a meeting at the gates,
where I pass through in the company of the Gods.
My soul is written upon Their faces of the sky,
as They rise through the worlds on their ladder,
my ladder that breaks the darkness of the vault,
as it receives the wings of those sacred spirits,
my ladder that stretches between the worlds,
lifting my name high above my worldly bones,
my ladder that speaks the names of those Gods
that hold my life for my meeting at the gates.

39: I Slay Death In His Field
Where They Begin Again

I turn into this field from which living men wander,
for theirs are dreams of pleasures without end,
senses ever filled like a summer sky with swallows,
their wings beating with the history of the sky,
while the corpses of the Earth are kept by the Earth,
and all that belongs to the soil returns to feed it.
This is what I am, and what you are, and what we are,
meeting the Earth again after our journey,
where there is never again a thing to fear.

Do you know why swallows never tarry on the ground?
Theirs is a home in the bosom of the sky,
or on the other side of vast oceans uncrossable to others.
But they cross them without a care for the wind,
wild and tumultuous like the desires of living men.
They cross without the comforts of Spring,
or the blankets of the willow sweeping the green.
Theirs is a pilgrimage between earth and wind,
to the eaves of the sky where they begin again.

Shall I now begin again as I make this field my home?
Ancient Father has given me His strength,
as I traversed the peaks of lonely mountains
where crows gathered.
And they gave to me their song and their joy,
not only the sorrows of the silent graves forgotten.
For the dead are my dead, and I shall be with them too,
to speak through the living stones of the empty valleys,
to sing through brook and meadow.
The dead are your dead also, and they are what we are.

Shall I now begin again as I make this sky my home?
Starry Mother has given my eyes their sight as I wandered
beneath the Bull's Thigh and his companions of light.
And they gave to me their map of the soul,
not only their ether where spirits are scattered.
For the stars are my spirit, and I shall be with them too,
to speak through the rising and falling of the brilliant veil,
to whisper through north and south.
The stars are your stars also, and they are what we are.

I turn from this earth over which living men wander,
to find pleasures and senses that can never be filled,
green youth that fades, riches and praise,
that stand for as long as a blade of grass stands.
They are all cut down by that indomitable wind
that drives the swallows before him.
This is what I am, and what you are, and what we are,
meeting the sky again after our journey,
where there is never again a thing to fear.

Do you know why stars never tarry in the sky?
Theirs is a home in the infinite directions,
or on the vault's other shore in company with souls.
But they return to the place where they began,
where the veil holds a gate in Her golden loins.
And this is the gate where living men aspire
to cross the threshold between flesh and air.
Theirs is a pilgrimage between earth and wind,
to the eaves of the sky where they begin again.

Shall I now begin again as I make this river my home?
The holy waters have given my spirit a current as I drifted
between the banks of yesterday and the morrow.
And they gave to me their wisdom of the present,
not only their memories where the past is scattered.
For memory is my eternal ladder, and I shall climb it too,
to speak through the language passed down by mothers,
to speak through the words the trees tell their sons.
Memories are your language also, and they are what we are.

Shall I now begin again as I make the wind my home?
The four directions have given my name a lasting power,
as I turn into this earth where I slay death in his field.
And they gave to me their names of the Ancient Gods,
not only the god of the fresh and fleeting present.
For the Gods of past are my future,
and I shall be with Them too,
to shout down through the ages where the many travel,
to wake up the sleeping Earth with the voice of its sky.
The Gods are your awakening also, and They are what we
are.

40: *Invested With A Door In the Sky*

I am invested with a pomegranate tree,
whose fruit of ruddy treasures tells the seasons.
Its ruby seeds foretell the sunset of my passions,
erupting as the fire of youth on love's horizon.
These I freely bestow in a garden pregnant with music,
unfolding from my hands with the climax of the Sun.
I have not hoarded the benevolence of this sacred tree,
but have given its fruit to the hungry lips abounding.
They now eat with me in a garden of peace abiding.

I am invested with a desert of khamsin winds,
howling through the peaks of the dying West.
This the direction all breathing men fear,
the keeper of my corpse when I abandon my vessel.
These are the sands I share with my brothers,
who partake of the mountain winds we haunt.
I have not possessed the vessel in which I moved,
but have given its stream to my thirsty brothers abounding.
They now move with me through the towers of the sky.

I am invested with a river of generous flood,
making its way through a barren land thirsting.
For me it has quenched the longing of my youth,
sweet with the dance of sycamores at dawn.
These are the green things I plant with my footfall,
wherever I am led by this river flowing from me.
I have not squandered the well from which I drank,
but have given its sweetness to the empty souls drifting.
They now drink with me between the banks of the earth.

I am invested with a net of brilliant gold,
spread across the sky for the bounty of the Sun.
Its warp is the past and its weft is the future,
foretold by a spangling of stars from which the Gods shine.
These are the maps I read with knowing eyes,
claiming the northern sky enduring for my spirit.
I have not shut out these lamps the Gods hung,
but have given their lights meaning in my deeds.
They now speak for the Gods in the wake of my travels.

I am invested with a torch in evening's garden,
blazing near a pool of flowers whose colors whisper.
They tell me the stories of sparrows climbing the sky,
of twilights that open their thighs for hunting moon.
These are the signs of life my heart has read,
lit by all the lights that Heaven knows.
I have not thrown away the knowledge of this garden,
but have cherished its flowers as the memory of the night.
They now unfold their petals for the day
when night has closed.

I am invested with a heart of red jasper,
whose voice is the call of a heron in its flight.
He alights in a willow as the Sun-God is swallowed,
and rises in the fire of dawn with a mantle of gold.
These are the tokens of renewal beyond the grave,
claimed by hearts in possession of a malachite edge.
I have not blunted these treasures of the turquoise sky,
but have planted them in the earth for others passing by.
They now take up my mantle through the winding world.

I am invested with a body of light,
coming forth by day from the corpse I have known.
He takes up other senses when the sky becomes him,
and Earth becomes his shadow as the eastern gate opens.
These are the Mysteries unknown to walking men,
who find the door held open when their skin falls silent.
I have not fled from the silence of this moment,
but have gathered all these treasures in my waking time.
They now hold open the sky for me,
through my nighttime travels.

I am invested with a door in the sky,
opening for my shadow as the Sun casts its magic.
Before it stands yesterday and behind it tomorrow,
roaring the future like twin lions in the veil.
These are the prophecies of flesh and their Spirit,
both walking on through the passage death keeps.
I have not averted my path from Spirit's journey,
but have walked toward that door with its messages in me.
They now speak through the door to the world in my wake.

41: Divine Beloved
There Was A Well and I Reached

There was a date palm and I reached for its fruit.
Glistening like jewels, that fruit woke my purpose,
and memories of a sweet elixir drew my feet on.
How the desert had chased my heart from its contentment,
longing for that distant valley,
swaying with malachite fronds.
My heart grew a stride
that measured the distance of mountains.
It could never be at peace with the wilderness it had known,
the grave for my flesh and the earth for my bone.
Will the quest of any pilgrim rest before reaching home?

Give me my feet to walk, and I will walk Your desert.
Breaking open the mountains with its breath,
my ears wake up to those powers above our heads
where we listen to the Gods
as They pass down Their memories,
where the forms of men are fashioned in the sacral fire.

There was a tamarisk and I reached for its honey.
Spun like thread of gold, its luster woke my courage,
a taste of that yonder valley clad in green memories.
"You will be led by the mettle of your hidden heart,"
this is what the tamarisk placed on the tip of my tongue,
which hungered for knowledge to the very reaches of the sky.

And it was the changing sky
that gave my heart its resilient metal,
a color that remains while all others change.
Will the heart of any pilgrim
let tarnished mettle lead the way?

Give me my lips to kiss, and I will kiss Your sky.
Casting its net of gold and precious stones,
my eyes wake up to that river above our heads,
where we swim with the Gods as They ride the wind,
where the souls of men endure as the halos of stars.

There was a well and I reached for sweet waters.
Reflecting the sapphire sky, that blue ocean woke my voice,
and songs of past travels drew my breath on.
How those restless spirits led my will from its complacency,
thirsty for the chorus of ancient and hallowed mouths,
my ears grew a reach exceeding the fiery horizons.
They could never be complacent
with the prattle they had known,
the mundane for my heart and the transitory for my soul.
Will the breath of any pilgrim rest before reaching home?

Give me my voice to speak, and I will speak Your names.
Resounding through the ages as the language of souls,
my mouth wakes up to that sound above our heads
where we speak with the Gods as They pronounce creation,
where the future of men is woven with the Sacred thread.

There was an acacia and I reached for its thorns.
Mirroring the cruel sands, those spears woke my senses,
and memories of my sufferings drew my endurance on.
How those barbs of the world urged my Spirit from its skin,
starving for the arms of my Beloved clad in sacred sky,
my image grew wings that spanned worldly chasms.
They could never alight
on the ephemeral pleasures they had known,
skin deep for my hands and shallow for my soul.
Will the vessel of any pilgrim rest before reaching home?

Give me my wings to fly, and I will fly to Your sky.
Opening through the veil of death and life,
my form of Spirit wakes up to that sound above our heads,
where we rise with the Gods as They raise creation,
where the love of men is liberated by the Sacred thread.

There was a torch and I reached for its fire.
Burning without air, its light woke my enduring sight,
and memories of my birth drew my Spirit on.
How the hands of death pulled my memory from its skin.
Gasping for the breath of my Beloved,
exhaling sacred sky,
my heart grew a memory that spanned the ages.
He could never find life in a single body he had known,
mortal in flesh and temporal of bone.
Will the soul of any pilgrim rest before reaching home?

42: Sacred Marriage
I Will Light More of Them

I stand at the threshold of the sky,
where sorrow passes through my feet
like a summer breeze.
These tears of mine add misery to the waters,
and yet I am never carried away with them.
This is the boon my mother gave me,
who comes with her head
covered in a shawl of tenderness,
like the red of a cardinal's wing.
Her shawl frames eyes and lips,
beaming with that light I know as hope.

You pass me a scarf on the wind,
and it is like my mother's hair.
She is a wanderer,
but she returns to me in my dreams,
to tell me all is well.
And is it well?

When I hear the thunder in the distance,
the sound chases my heart into the shadows.
And there I wait with the spirits of my memories,
who whisper prayers louder than thunder,
who light candles beaming with that light
I know as compassion.

And I will light more of them,
for my brothers shimmering now behind the veil.
And I will light more of them,
for my sisters dancing now behind the veil.
And that veil is like my mother's hair,
which covers my sorrows as they tell a tale
from behind my light's veil.

I meet tenderness beneath a tree,
with spirals reaching out from the bosom of that sky,
where death passes through my hands
like a stream moved by Spring.
These moments of beauty and pleasure
add life to the waters,
and yet I am never carried away with them.
This is the boon my father gave me,
who comes with his eyes hidden in a cloak of darkness.
Like the black of a raven's breast,
his cloak shields heart and hands,
enduring with that spirit
I know as time.

You pass me a candle on the Moon,
and it is like my father's voice.
He is a wanderer,
but he returns to me in my dreams
to tell me all is well.
And is it well?

When I hear grieving in the distance,
the sound chases my heart into the shadows.
And there I wait with the music of my memories,
who whispers joy louder than our sorrows,
who lights candles beaming with that light
I know as solace.
And I will light more of them
for my lovers shimmering now behind the veil.
And I will light more of them
for my family dancing now behind the veil.
And that veil is like my mother's hair,
which covers my sorrows as they tell a tale
from behind my light's veil.

About the Author

Ptahmassu K.M. Nofra-Uaa is an internationally noted iconographer whose celebrated work has been featured in publications including *Softpower Magazine* and best-selling author Nicki Scully's book *Sekhmet, Transformation in the Belly of the Goddess.* His icons are highly coveted by individuals and institutions, so much so that the waiting list for new commissions is nearly four years long. He is a sought-after speaker for podcasts and publications with a polytheist perspective, and has influenced international artists who credit him with having compelled their Kemetic or magical inspirations.

His work has also been lauded by professional Egyptologists for its unique yet authentic voice.

He is the founder of *Icons of Kemet*, dedicated to the crafting of unique God-images for use in worship of the ancient Gods of Egypt. A spokesperson for devotional polytheism, his poetic hymns have been published in the volumes of *Neos Alexandria/Bibliotheca Alexandrina, Lord of the Carnelian Temple, A Devotional In Honour of Sobek* (2018), and *A Silver Sun and Inky Clouds, the Devotional Anthology for Djehuty and Set* (2018). He is a priest of the Temple of Isis, California, a legally recognized sanctuary of the Goddess Isis in the United States, and a Priest-Hierophant in the international Fellowship of Isis, whose aims include the celebration of the Egyptian Goddess Isis and related Goddess traditions from around the globe.

As a speaker and writer on various aspects of devotional polytheism, Ptahmassu's work has been featured in *Isian News, the Official Newsletter of the Fellowship of Isis*, and in *Isis-Seshat, A Quarterly Journal of the Fellowship of Isis*. His works of poetry and prose manifest from his continued mission to serve the ancient Gods as living Gods, and in so doing to encourage others in the rehabilitation and revival of humankind's polytheistic religious traditions.

To learn more about the author and his work, readers are invited to visit his official website and blog,

www.iconsofkmt.com
www.scribe.iconsofkmt.com

About the Cover Art

Ptahmassu K.M. Nofra-Uaa
Pazuzu the Divine Exorcist, ©2014,
8" x 10" wood panel
semi-precious mineral watercolor,
22 karat gold, amethyst, lapis lazuli

All praise to You Pazuzu Son of Hanbi,
King of Wind Demons, the victorious,
Lord of terror in the South,
Master of storms in the West,
Bearer of victory Who is undefeated.

Great Lord, bringing with Him the shuddering
Of the dark sky,
Fill for me the heavens
With glorious strength!
Receive my prayer,
Stretch its fury through the sky
With the lightning of Your divine hand.
Bring my enemies to justice,
But bring no harm to my house
Or those dwelling within its grace.

Lord of demons whose fury
Knows the boundaries of the four directions,
Grant unto me the shield of Your glory,
And may my prayers be exalted by the
Great Gods of the skies!

O Pazuzu, Son of Hanbi, terrible and feared,
all praise to You, when in Your valor You
appear in the South!
The earth quakes in Your footsteps,
the winds obey Your commands,
hearts shudder, awe overtakes the world!

O Pazuzu, come forth to protect, not to harm.
Receive this offering of my heart,
and may my home be protected from all sources of harm.
Raise your mighty right arm,
encircle the boundaries of my dwelling,
drive back my enemies, safeguard all that I love.

O Pazuzu, You are the most terrible
Son of Hanbi, Whom the Gods-
even in their greatness- fear above all.
No injustice escapes Your wrath, which is great,
but so too is Your mercy great,
which shapes mountains and wind
to accomplish its will!

Praise to You, O Pazuzu the Great!
Come to do good, never ill.
Come to help, and never to harm.
Come to bless, and never to curse me.
May the Earth receive Your mighty feet,
and the winds obey the holy touch of
Your divine hand!

-Prayer of Invocation to Pazuzu by Ptahmassu Nofra-Uaa

Pazuzu was both venerated and feared within the pantheons of the Mesopotamians, Assyrians and Babylonians, and functioned from His very beginnings as an apotropaic domestic spirit-deity, whose spheres of influence were especially bound to the protection of the home from malign influences and hostile personages.

As a controller of the often unruly winds, and the noxious spirits that were known to dwell within them, Pazuzu is hailed as the king of the wind-demons, meaning to the ancients that He had ultimate power over the machinations of these beings and the element in which they dwelt. It was specifically the southwestern wind to which Pazuzu was assigned, though his authority extends not only to the four winds of creation, but also to mountains (which he may cause to quake) and weather patterns.

On the domestic front Pazuzu behaves as a guardian of the household from all unwanted visitors, which include evil spirits and murderous demons, but most especially those who seek to harm women in childbirth, infants and children. In this role Pazuzu is recognized as the one magical, spiritual source that can be summoned to defend mothers and infants from the murderous demoness Lamashtu, whose special prey are newborns and young children.

It was the head of Pazuzu that was most frequently used by the ancients to invoke his magical power and terrifying apotropaic nature, believed to be resident in the blend of leonine and canid features. Pazuzu's forehead is characterized by deep wrinkles, thick eyebrows and a pair of horns, which most probably represented his divine nature and power to the ancient

Mesopotamians, who depicted their most powerful deities with crowns featuring long horns curling back from the forehead. His undernourished chest with prominent ribs is another hallmark feature of Pazuzu's body, which has leonine hands with claws, leonine ankles, eagle's talons and a raised scorpion tail.

Pazuzu's gesture, with upraised right hand and lowered, splayed left hand, is characteristic of Near Eastern deities of martial and environmental potency, where upraised right arms and/ or fists denote destruction of enemies and removal of adversaries or obstacles. In his position as controller and vanquisher of demons and hostile forces, Pazuzu's defensive stance, including striding left leg, signals his ferocious, combative nature, ever ready to govern the unruly and strike down the forces that attack the weak or defenseless. As the king of the West wind and its inhabitants, Pazuzu sprouts two pairs of eagle's wings.

Symbols of the other almighty gods with whom Pazuzu was sometimes associated are also depicted in this icon. Above Pazuzu's head soars the orb of the solar sovereign and justice-maker Shamash, which has been combined with the winged disk of the high god Ashur, into which has been placed the eight-pointed star of the goddess Ishtar (from whose center sparkles a Brazilian amethyst). All of these symbols are to be found on apotropaic plaques used in rituals to defeat the feared demoness Lamashtu, over whom Pazuzu was believed to wield magical control and persuasive acumen.

Combined with the insurmountable authority and justice of the very high gods and goddesses, Pazuzu makes His appearance on such ceremonial objects in order to defeat the demons (and in particular Lamashtu) that use the cover of darkness to afflict hapless women and children. The crescent moon of the lunar god Sin is also present in a night sky swirling with the forceful southwestern winds through which Pazuzu's awesome power is made manifest. The lightning bolt of the storm god Adad, which is embellished with cabochons of lapis lazuli from Afghanistan, flanks both sides of the icon panel.

The colors used for this icon are derived from the very bright glazed tiles found on such monuments as the fabulous Ishtar Gate of Babylon and the palace of king Darius I at Susa, which preserves some of the most vivid representations from the Babylonian religious iconographic repertoire. The icon panel, together with the gilded jewelry worn by the deity, honors the Mesopotamian roots of Pazuzu by referencing the designs seen in Mesopotamian and Assyrio-Babylonian regalia.

Each icon that is brought to life by Ptahmassu Nofra-Uaa is the outcome of an intense process of sacred initiation involving direct contact with a goddess or god through meditation and dream incubation, and it is these, paired with intense research and devotion, that guides the creative hand of the iconographer. Each icon is crafted using the finest natural mineral pigments, gold, semi-precious and precious stones, and is ritually awakened and blessed before installation in a temple or shrine.

About Icons of Kemet

'Hail to you Ptah, Lord of Life of the Two Lands.
I have come before you, that I may worship you.
I am a servant who does not forget his duty
in your festivals, truly!'

-Inscription from the stela of the washerman
Hepet. 13th Dynasty.

R.B. Parker. Voices From Ancient Egypt, An
Anthology of Middle Kingdom Writings, 128.

Since its inception in 2011 by iconographer Ptahmassu Nofra-Uaa, Icons of Kemet has been a voice for devotional polytheism and the values of Kemeticism, the veneration of the Goddesses and Gods of ancient Egypt today. Part and parcel of this veneration is the establishment of sacred spaces where the Natcharu (Netjeru or Gods) may be worshiped in Their images. Such images come in many forms, both three and two-dimensional representations, and are used to draw and maintain the presences of the Gods in sacred space. Icons of Kemet was envisaged as a forum for the creation of holy images that would satisfy this need for divine representation in sacred space, while also serving as a vehicle for ritual activities and services traditional to the adoration of the Gods of Kemet.

The works promoted by Icons of Kemet are fueled by a framework of ritual activities authentic to the ancient Egyptian traditions. God-images are crafted according to a lunar schedule, with each aspect of the work being initiated at the appropriate lunar phase or festival: prayers and Utterances taken directly from the Daily Cult texts and other source texts are recited at each stage in the production of an image; pilgrimage is made with each image in progress to holy sites established in the desert landscape of the iconographer, here to receive feeding with offerings and veneration by way of traditional liturgies and acts; natural semi-precious mineral pigments, gold, platinum, precious and semi-precious stones are used in the creation of each God-image. The final act in activating a God-image occurs with the Mouth Opening Ritual conducted with the original texts and instruments made according to traditional materials and practices.

Icons of Kemet icons or God-images are not mere copies of preexisting ancient works, nor are they fantastical projections of the artist's mind. What makes the icons of Icons of Kemet unique devotional works is their following of traditional canon, iconography, and religious practices without directly copying what has been crafted before. These are masterpieces of the highest technical skill composed of the finest materials, not as works of art that express an artist's personal experiences, but as divinely possessed cult-images that serve as the focal point for a religious community's spiritual life.